Funny

AMIGURUMI

★ 16 CREATURES & THEIR ACCESSORIES ★
TO CROCHET

Emilie Penou

stashBOOKS®

an imprint of C&T Publishing

ACKNOWLEDGEMENTS

· Felted mushroom: **MUSHKANE**

· Castle, kitchen, small suitcase, cart, tipi and tent: **MAILEG**

· Cardboard, tiny wooden boxes, glue, scissors and glitters: **ROUGIER & PLÉ**

IMPERIAL CONVERSIONS

The imperial measurements in this book follow standard conversion practices for sewing and soft crafts. The imperial equivalents are often rounded off for ease of use. If you need more exact measurements, there are a number of amazing online converters.

Funny Amigurumi

First published in the United States in 2023 by Stash Books, an imprint of C&T Publishing, Inc., P.O. Box 1456, Lafayette, CA 94549

Amigurumis amusants © 2020 by Éditions Marie Claire - Société d'Information et de Créations (SIC)

This edition of "Amigurumis amusants" first published in France by Éditions Marie Claire in 2020 is published by arrangement with Marie Claire.

PUBLISHER: Amy Barrett-Daffin

CREATIVE DIRECTOR: Gailen Runge

SENIOR EDITOR: Roxane Cerda

EDITORS: Jennifer Warren and Madison Moore

ENGLISH-LANGUAGE COVER DESIGNER: April Mostek

ENGLISH TRANSLATION: Eliette Pebay-Maes

PRODUCTION COORDINATOR: Zinnia Heinzmann

Printed in China

10 9 8 7 6 5 4 3 2

Funny
AMIGURUMI

CONTENTS

INTRODUCTION

10 CROCHET LESSONS

16 AMIGURUMI PATTERNS

PAGE 20

PAGE 24

PAGE 28

PAGE 32

1. MS. MINI BUNNY
AND CARROT

2. MR. MINI BUG
AND APHID

3. MR. MINI TIGER
AND BOWTIE

4. MR. MINI FOX
AND MASK

10 CROCHET LESSONS

TECHNIQUES

CH (CHAIN):

Make a slip knot on the hook, yarn over, then draw the loop through the original loop. Yarn over again, and pull the loop through the stitch. Repeat as many times as needed to get the right number of stitches. When making your first single crochet row after a chain, always hook into the second stitch from the hook unless specified otherwise, in which case explanations will be given in the pattern.

SC (SINGLE CROCHET):

Insert your hook into the next stitch, yarn over then pull the loop through the stitch. Yarn over again, then pull through both loops, slipping them off the hook.

SL ST (SLIP STITCH):

Insert the hook into the next stitch, yarn over, then pull the loop through the two loops on the hook.

CSC (CENTER SINGLE CROCHET):

Insert the hook into the 'V' of the next stitch, yarn over, then pull the loop through the stitch. Yarn over again, then pull through both loops, slipping them off the hook.

HDC (HALF DOUBLE CROCHET):

Yarn over, insert your hook into the next stitch, yarn over then pull the loop through the stitch. You now have three stitches on the hook. Yarn over again, then pull through all three loops.

DC (DOUBLE CROCHET).

Yarn over, insert the hook into the next stitch, yarn over, then pull the loop through the stitch. You now have three loops on the hook. Yarn over again, pull through the first two loops, yarn over one last time, then pull through the last two loops.

BO (BOBBLE STITCH):

Yarn over, insert the hook into the stitch in the previous row, yarn over, pull the loop through the stitch, yarn over, then pull the yarn through two loops; you now have two loops on the hook.

Yarn over, insert the hook into the same stitch as before, yarn over, pull the loop through the stitch, yarn over, then pull the yarn through two loops; you now have three loops on the hook.

Yarn over, insert the hook into the same stitch as before, yarn over, pull the loop through the stitch, yarn over, then pull the yarn through two loops; you now have four loops on the hook. Yarn over, insert the hook into the same stitch as before, yarn over, pull the loop through the stitch, yarn over, then pull the yarn through two loops; you now have five loops on the hook. To finish, yarn over and pull it through all five loops on the hook.

PICOT:

Chain three stitches, then make a slip stitch in the back of the first chain stitch (in the bump).

INC. (INCREASE):

2 SC into the same stitch.

DCINC (DOUBLE CROCHET INCREASE):

2 DC into the same stitch.

DEC. (INVISIBLE DECREASE):

All decreases in this book are invisible decreases. Insert the hook in the front loop of the first stitch, then, without yarning over, insert it in the front loop of the second stitch. Once both stitches are on the hook, yarn over and pull through both loops. Yarn over again and pull through the last two loops.

... X:

Repeat the instructions in between the asterisks (*) as many times as specified by the value represented by 'X'.

(COLOR):

Indicates that starting from this row, you will be crocheting with the color given in parenthesis.

{STITCHES}:

Indicates that the stitches between { } must be made from the same stitch.

FL (FRONT LOOP) / BL (BACK LOOP):

Indicates in which loop the row must be crocheted.

THE MAGIC RING

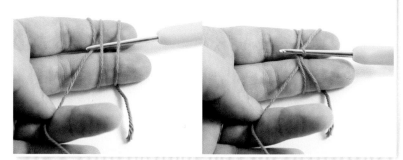

1 Wrap the yarn three times around your fingers, with its tail on the right.

2 Slip the hook under the first two strands and grab the third strand (the one that is connected to the skein), then bring that strand under the first two.

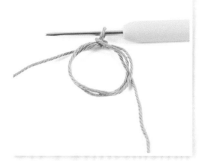
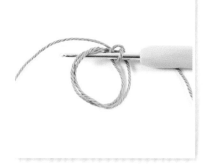

3 Yarn over, then pull the yarn through the loop.

4 Carefully remove the ring from your fingers.

5 Now, single crochet six stitches by inserting the hook inside the ring to grab the yarn.

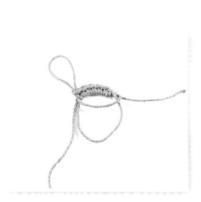

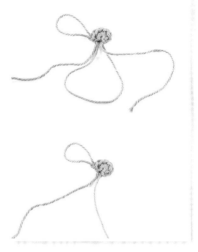

6 After completing six single crochet stitches, pull on the loop that's on the hook so that you won't lose it, and remove the hook (this loop will not be used for Steps 8–10).

7 Lightly pull on the yarn pictured on the right (the tail) and watch the two loops in the middle to see which one gets smaller.

8 When you know which loop is shrinking, pull on it until the other one closes up completely. You now have only one loop left in the middle. Pull on the tail yarn to close the remaining loop in the middle.

9 Start working the piece (and the loop you set aside) by doing your first single crochet stitch into the first stitch on the magic ring.

10 Here is what it looks like.

PAGE 46

Mr. Unicorn

WRONG SIDE OR RIGHT SIDE?

How to tell the right side from the wrong side when working in the round:

1 On the right side of a piece worked in the round, you can see the 'V' of each stitch.

2 On the wrong side of a piece worked in the round, you can see the horizontal loops in the back of each stitch.

CHANGING COLORS IN THE ROUND

There are many techniques that allow you to change colors in the round. Here is the one I use, that I find simple and efficient:

1 Close your round with the invisible stitch (page 11) and make a slip knot on the hook with the new color.

2 Insert the hook into the last stitch of the previous round (usually a slip stitch) and single crochet one stitch. Then keep working the round by stitching into those you've created while making the invisible finish.

3 You will get a new round of a different color with an almost invisible seam.

INVISIBLE FINISH IN THE ROUND

You are ready for the invisible finish when your round is done and you've closed it with a slip stitch.

1 Skip the next stitch (the one after the slip stitch), and work into the second stitch (as shown by the hook).

2 Bring the hook under the V of the stitch.

3 See above for the correct placement.

4 Go back and insert the hook in the middle of the stitch your yarn comes from (the slip stitch).

5 This creates a stitch which superposes itself onto the stitch you skipped in Step 2. Bring in the yarn without pulling too tight.

FINISHING TECHNIQUES

SINGLE LAYER FINISH

A single layer finish creates a nice and tight finishing row when there are no clearly identifiable stitches.

1 Make a slip knot on the hook with the yarn you want to use for the edging.

2 Look closely at the row on the side of your work. You will crochet once into the front loop of the stitch, once into the bump, and then continue in the same way (front loop, bump, etc.).

3 Here is what it looks like.

TWO-LAYER FINISH (JOINING)

1 Take the pieces you need to crochet together and place their wrong sides together, their right sides facing out.

2 Insert the hook under the 'V' of the stitch through both layers. You will have four loops on the hook.

3 Single crochet one stitch, then continue that way all around your work (making increases if directed).

CENTER SINGLE CROCHET
AND COLOR CHANGE

1 Crochet up to one stitch before the color change.

2 Insert the hook into the 'V' of the next stitch.

3 Yarn over.

4 With two loops of the first color on the hook, yarn over with the second color and pull it through the stitches.

5 Then continue the row with the second color as directed. Repeat Steps 1–4 at the next color change.

PAGE 70

Ms. Penguin

CROCHETING ARMS TO BODY

For the larger Amigurumis, you have the choice between sewing the arms to the body at the end, or crocheting the arms in as you're working the pattern. To crochet the arms as you work:

1 The body that's being worked on is blue, and the finished arm is orange. You are going to crochet the body and the arm simultaneously in order to secure them together.

2 Flatten the arm and insert the hook through both layers (two stitches).

3 Then insert the hook into the body, following the pattern instructions. You now have three stitches on the hook, which will make your work quite stiff. Single crochet one stitch.

PAGE 70

Ms. Donkey

4 You have attached the beginning of the arm. Repeat Steps 2–3 all along the arm.

HAIR

1 Cut strands of yarn, following the pattern's instructions for length.

2 Insert the hook in the amigurumi's head, body or tail, or under a stitch as indicated in the pattern. Depending on which way you want the hairs to flow, you will insert the hook upward, downward, right-left or left-right.

3 Grab the middle of the yarn with the hook.

4 Pull it through the stitch.

5 Grab the two tail strands of yarn.

6 Pull them through the loop on the hook. Repeat those steps as many times as needed.

MANES

1 Make a chain with as many stitches as required by the pattern, then insert the hook through a stitch on the Amigurumi.

2 Grab the yarn and make a slip stitch.

3 Here is what it looks like. The chain is now secured to the unicorn's head.

Mr. Unicorn

PAGE 46

4 Then, slip stitch down the length of the chain.

TENTACLES

1 Work directly after the previous golden row (Mr. Squid pattern, body instructions). Fold your work to see the stitch on the edge of row 27, where you'll insert the hook. The blue part (row 29) is on the bottom of the tentacle.

2 Insert the hook into the edge stitch, from the outside in.

3 Single crochet one stitch.

PAGE 90

Mr. Squid

4 Single crochet all five stitches and notice the stitch on the edge of row 26, which will allow you to finish row 30.

5 Insert the hook into the edge stitch, from the inside out, to make a single crochet stitch, and continue this for the whole tentacle.

16 AMIGURUMI PATTERNS

MS. MINI BUNNY AND CARROT

LEVEL: BEGINNER

SIZE: 6˝ (15cm)

MATERIALS

- Hook size D/3 (3mm) or whatever matches your yarn, if using a different kind
- Scheepjes Catona Cotton yarn (100% mercerized cotton) or similar yarn:

    1 skein in white (main color), approx. 65 yards (60m)

    1 skein in orange, approx. 10 yards (10m)

    1 skein in green, approx. 7 yards (7m)

    1 pink strand

- Two 6mm safety eyes (or black embroidery cotton yarn)
- Stuffing
- Tapestry needle
- Scissors

TECHNIQUES USED

- ch (chain)
- sc (single crochet)
- sl st (slip stitch)
- inc. (increase)
- dec. (invisible decrease)
- magic ring (page 8)

NOTES

1 This amigurumi is crocheted in the round, unless specified otherwise.

2 If this stuffed animal is for a child, go down one hook size if you crochet loosely.

3 If this stuffed animal is for an infant, replace the safety eyes with embroidered eyes.

INSTRUCTIONS

HEAD AND BODY

In white

Rnd 1: Start with a magic ring

Rnd 2: 6 sc in MR (6 st)

Rnd 3: inc. in all 6 stitches (12 st)

Rnd 4: *1 sc, inc.* x 6 (18 st)

Rnd 5: 1 sc, inc., *2 sc, inc.* x 5, 1 sc (24 st)

Rnd 6: *3 sc, inc.* x 6 (30 st)

Rnd 7: SC in each stitch around (30 st)

Rnd 8: 2 sc, inc., *4 sc, inc.* x 5, 2 sc (36 st)

Rnd 9: SC in each stitch around (36 st)

Rnd 10: *5 sc, inc.* x 6 (42 st)

Rnd 11–26: SC in each stitch around (42 st)

Insert the eyes between round 10 and 11 with 7 stitches in between. Start stuffing.

Rnd 27: *5sc, dec.* x 6 (36 st)

Rnd 28: SC in each stitch around (36 st)

Rnd 29: 2 sc, dec., *4 sc, dec.* x 5, 2 sc (30 st)

Rnd 30: *3 sc, dec.* x 6 (24 st)

Rnd 31: 1 sc, dec., 2 sc, dec.* x 5, 1 sc (18 st)

Rnd 32: *1 sc, dec.* x 6 (12 st)
Rnd 33: Dec 6 times. (6 st)
Stuff tightly. Cut the yarn and weave it through the remaining 6 stitches using a tapestry needle, pull tight and weave it in. Embroider the nose with a strand of pink yarn 2 rounds below the eyes.

EARS

In white

Rnd 1: Start with a magic ring
Rnd 2: 4 sc in MR (4 st)
Rnd 3: Inc in all 4 stitches. (8 st)
Rnd 4: *1 sc, inc.* x 4 (12 st)
Rnds 5–14: SC in each stitch around (12 st)
Rnd 15: *1 sc, dec.* x 4 (8 st)
No stuffing necessary. Finish with 1 sl st. Cut the yarn, leaving enough length for sewing. Make the second ear the same way.

ARMS

In white

Rnd 1: Start with a magic ring
Rnd 2: 6 sc in MR (6 st)
Rnd 3: *1 sc, inc.* x 3 (9 st)
Rnds 4–9: SC in each stitch around (9 st)
Rnd 10: *1 sc, dec.* x 3 (6 st)
Stuff lightly. Cut the yarn, leaving enough length for sewing, and weave it through the remaining 6 stitches using a tapestry needle. Pull tight. Make the second arm the same way.

LEGS

In white

Rnd 1: Start with a magic ring
Rnd 2: 4 sc in MR (4 st)
Rnd 3: Inc in all 4 stitches (8 st)
Rnd 4: SC in each stitch around (8 st)
Rnd 5: *1 sc, inc.* x 4 (12 st)
Rnds 6–9: SC in each stitch around (12 st)
Start stuffing
Rnd 10: *1 sc, dec.* x 4 (8 st)
Rnd 11: 8 st
Stuff lightly. Cut the yarn, leaving enough length for sewing, and weave it through the remaining 8 stitches using a tapestry needle. Pull tight. Embroider the bottom of the paw with a strand of pink yarn.
Make the second leg the same way.

The ears

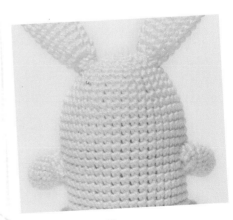

The arms

The tail

The carrot

THE TAIL

In white

Rnd 1: Start with a magic ring
Rnd 2: 6 sc in MR (6 st)
Rnd 3: Inc in all 6 stitches. (12 st)
Rnd 4: *1 sc, inc.* x 6 (18 st)
Start stuffing
Rnds 5–6: SC in each stitch around (18 st)
Rnd 7: *1 sc, dec.* x 6 (12 st)
Stuff tightly, finish with 1 sl st, then cut the yarn leaving enough length for sewing.

FINISHING

Sew the ears to the head. Fold the ears in half at the base to give them a hollow look and sew them between rows 4 and 6.
Sew the arms to the body between rows 16 and 20.
Sew the legs to the body around row 31.
Sew the tail to the body between rows 24 and 29.

CARROT

THE CONE

In orange

Rnd 1: Start with a magic ring
Rnd 2: 6 sc in MR (6 st)
Rnd 3: Inc in all 6 stitches (12 st)
Rnds 4–6: SC in each stitch around (12 st)
Rnd 7: *4 sc, dec.* x 2 (10 st)
Rnds 8–9: SC in each stitch around (10 st)
Rnd 10: *3 sc, dec.* x 2 (8 st)
Start stuffing
Rnds 11–12: SC in each stitch around (8 st)
Rnd 13: *2 sc, dec.* x 2 (6 st)
Rnd 14: SC in each stitch around (6 st)
Rnd 15: Dec. 3 times (3 st)
Stuff tightly. Cut the yarn and weave it through the remaining 3 stitches using a tapestry needle, pull tight and weave it in.

THE LEAVES

In green

Rnd 1: Start with a magic ring
Rnd 2: 4 sc in MR (4 st)
Rnd 3: 1 sl st in the 1st sc, 5 ch. Starting from the 2nd chain from the hook, sl st in the next 4 chains, finish with another sl st in the 1st sc.
1 sl st in the 2nd sc, 6 ch. Starting from the 2nd chain from the hook, sl st in the next 5 chains, finish with another sl st in 2nd sc.
1 sl st in the 3rd sc, 4 ch. Starting from the 2nd chain from the hook, sl st in next 3 chains, finish with another sl st in 3rd sc.
1 sl st in the 4th sc, 8 ch. Starting from the 2nd chain from the hook, sl st in next 7 chains, finish with another sl st in 4th sc.
Cut the yarn, and finish by using the tail to sew the leaves to the top of the carrot.

MR. MINI BUG AND APHID

LEVEL: BEGINNER

SIZE: 4¼" (11cm)

MATERIALS

- Hook size D/3 (3mm) or whatever matches your yarn, if using a different kind
- Scheepjes Catona Cotton yarn (100% mercerized cotton) or similar yarn:

    1 skein in black (main color), approx. 75 yards (75m)

    1 skein in red, approx. 40 yards (40m)

    1 skein in white, approx. 30 yards (30m)

    1 skein in green, approx. 40 yards (40m)

- Two 6mm safety eyes (or black embroidery cotton yarn)
- Stuffing
- Tapestry needle
- Scissors

TECHNIQUES USED

- ch (chain)
- sc (single crochet)
- sl st (slip stitch)
- inc. (increase)
- dec. (invisible decrease)
- magic ring (page 8)

NOTES

1 This amigurumi is crocheted in the round, unless specified otherwise.

2 If this stuffed animal is for a child, go down one hook size if you crochet loosely.

3 If this stuffed animal is for an infant, replace the safety eyes with embroidered eyes.

INSTRUCTIONS

HEAD AND BODY

In black

Rnd 1: Start with a magic ring

Rnd 2: 6 sc in MR (6 st)

Rnd 3: Inc in all 6 stitches (12 st)

Rnd 4: *1 sc, inc.* x 6 (18 st)

Rnd 5: 1 sc, inc., *2 sc, inc.* x 5, 1 sc (24 st)

Rnd 6: *3 sc, inc.* x 6 (30 st)

Rnd 7: SC in each stitch around (30 st)

Rnd 8: 2 sc, inc., *4 sc, inc.* x 5, 2 sc (36 st)

Rnd 9: SC in each stitch around (36 st)

Rnd 10: *5 sc, inc.* x 6 (42 st)

Rnds 11–26: SC in each stitch around (42 st)

Insert the eyes between round 10 and 11 with 7 stitches in between.

Rnd 27: *5 sc, dec.* x 6 (36 st)

Rnd 28: SC in each stitch around (36 st)

Rnd 29: 2 sc, dec., *4 sc, dec.* x 5, 2 sc (30 st)

Start stuffing
Rnd 30: *3 sc, dec.* x 6 (24 st)
Rnd 31: 1 sc, dec., *2 sc, dec.* x 5, 1 sc (18 st)
Rnd 32: *1 sc, dec.* x 6 (12 st)
Rnd 33: Dec 6 times (6 st)
Stuff tightly. Cut the yarn and weave it through the remaining 6 stitches using a tapestry needle, pull tight and weave it in.

CHEEKS
In white
Rnd 1: Start with a magic ring
Rnd 2: 6 sc in MR (6 st)
Finish with 1 sl st, then cut the yarn leaving enough length for sewing. Make the second cheek the same way.

ANTENNAS
In black
Rnd 1: Start with a magic ring
Rnd 2: 6 sc in MR (6 st)

Rnd 3: SC in each stitch around (6 st)
Lightly stuff there.
Rnd 4: *1 sc, dec.* x 2 (4 st)
Rnds 5–6: SC in each stitch around (4 st)
Finish with 1 sl st, then cut the yarn leaving enough length for sewing. Make the second antenna the same way.

ARMS
In black
Rnd 1: Start with a magic ring
Rnd 2: 6 sc in MR (6 st)
Rnd 3: *1 sc, inc.* x 3 (9 st)
Rnds 4–9: SC in each stitch around (9 st)
Rnd 10: *1 sc, dec.* x 3 (6 st)
Stuff lightly. Cut the yarn leaving enough length for sewing and weave it through the remaining 6 stitches using a tapestry needle, pull tight. Make three more arms the same way.

LEGS
In black
Rnd 1: Start with a magic ring
Rnd 2: 6 sc in MR (6 st)
Rnd 3: Inc in all 6 stitches (12 st)
Rnd 4: [BACK LOOP] SC in each stitch around (12 st)
Rnd 5: SC in each stitch around (12 st)
Rnd 6: 3 sc, 3 dec., 3 sc (9 st)
Rnds 7–9: SC in each stitch around (9 st)
Rnd 10: *1 sc, dec.* x 3 (6 st)
Stuff tightly. Cut the yarn leaving enough length for sewing and weave it through the remaining 6 stitches using a tapestry needle, pull tight. Make the second leg the same way.

The cheeks

The wings

The wings

UNDER WINGS

Worked flat, in white.

Row 1: 3 ch, turn.
Row 2: 2 sc, 1 ch, turn. (2 st)
Row 3: 2 inc., 1 ch, turn (4 st)
Rows 4–6: 4 sc, 1 ch, turn
Row 7: inc., 2 sc, inc., 1 ch, turn (6 st)
Rows 8–12: 6 sc, 1 ch, turn
Row 13: inc., 4 sc, inc., 1 ch, turn (8 st)
Rows 14–19: 8 sc, 1 ch, turn
Row 20: dec., 4 sc, dec., 1 ch, turn (6 st)
Row 21: dec., 2 sc, dec., 1 ch, turn (4 st)
Row 22: 2 dec., 1 ch, turn (2 st)
End with a single crochet edge around the entire wing for a pretty finish. Sl st to the initial sc edge stitch, then cut the yarn and weave it in.
Repeat to make the second wing the same way.

TOP WINGS

In red

Rnd 1: Start with a magic ring
Rnd 2: 6 sc in MR (6 st)
Rnd 3: Inc in all 6 stitches (12 st)
Rnd 4: *1 sc, inc.* x 6 (18 st)
Rnd 5: 1 sc, inc., *2 sc, inc.* x 5, 1 sc (24 st)
Rnd 6: *3 sc, inc.* x 6 (30 st)
Rnd 7: 2 sc, inc., *4 sc, inc.* x 5, 2 sc (36 st)
Rnd 8: *5 sc, inc.* x 6 (42 st)
Rnd 9: 3 sc, inc., *6 sc, inc.* x 5, 3 sc (48 st)
Rnd 10: *7 sc, inc.* x 6 (54 st)
Rnd 11: 4 sc, inc., *8 sc, inc.* x 5, 4 sc (60 st)
Rnd 12: *9 sc, inc.* x 6 (66 st)
Fold the circle in half and make a single crochet row all around the edge, making sure to go through both layers. You'll get a red half-circle. Cut the yarn and weave it in.
Repeat to make the second wing the same way.

DOTS

In black

Rnd 1: Start with a magic ring
Rnd 2: 6 sc in MR (6 st)
Rnd 3: Inc in all 6 stitches (12 st)
Finish with 1 sl st, then cut the yarn leaving enough length for sewing.
Make six total, or as many as you want to decorate the wings.

Sew the antennas to the head between rows 4 and 5.
Sew the cheeks to the head between rows 12 and 14, close to the eyes.
Sew the arms to the body. The first set between rows 14 and 18 and the second set between rows 19 and 23.
Sew the black dots to the red wings.
Sew the white under wings and the red wings to the body. Sew the white wings first, vertically, with the top of the wing near row 8 and right against each other. Then cover them with the red wings, slightly apart from each other, near row 7.

APHID

In light green

Rnd 1: Start with a magic ring
Rnd 2: 6 sc in MR (6 st)
Rnd 3: Inc in all 6 stitches (12 st)
Rnds 4–5: SC in each stitch around (12 st)
Rnd 6: *1 sc, 1 inc.* x 6 (18 st)
Rnds 7–12: SC in each stitch around (18 st)
Rnd 13: *7 sc, dec.* x 2 (16 st)
Rnd 14: *6 sc, dec.* x 2 (14 st)
Rnd 15: *5 sc, dec.* x 2 (12 st)
Rnd 16: *4 sc, dec.* x 2 (10 st)
Rnd 17: *3 sc, dec.* x 2 (8 st)
Rnd 18: *2 sc, dec.* x 2 (6 st)
Stuff tightly. Cut the yarn and weave it through the remaining 6 stitches using a tapestry needle, pull tight and weave it in. Embroider the eyes with black yarn and use a simple light green strand of yarn to make the 6 legs and the antennas.

MR. MINI TIGER AND BOWTIE

LEVEL: BEGINNER

SIZE: 4¼″ (11cm)

MATERIALS

- Hook size D/3 (3mm) or whatever matches your yarn, if using a different kind
- Scheepjes Catona Cotton yarn (100% mercerized cotton) or similar yarn:

  1 skein in orange (main color), approx. 50 yards (50m)

  1 skein in black, approx. 10 yards (10m)

  1 skein in white, approx. 15 yards (15m)

- Two 6mm safety eyes (or black embroidery cotton yarn)
- Stuffing
- Tapestry needle
- Scissors

TECHNIQUES USED

- ch (chain)
- sc (single crochet)
- sl st (slip stitch)
- dc (double crochet)
- inc. (increase)
- dcinc (double crochet increase)
- dec. (invisible decrease)
- FL / BL (front loop / back loop)
- magic ring (page 8)

NOTES

1 This amigurumi is crocheted in the round, unless specified otherwise.

2 If this stuffed animal is for a child, go down one hook size if you crochet loosely.

3 If this stuffed animal is for an infant, replace the safety eyes with embroidered eyes.

INSTRUCTIONS

HEAD AND BODY

In orange

Rnd 1: Start with a magic ring
Rnd 2: 6 sc in MR (6 st)
Rnd 3: Inc in all 6 stitches (12 st)
Rnd 4: *1 sc, Inc.* x 6 (18 st)
Rnd 5: 1 sc, Inc., *2 sc, Inc.* x 5, 1 sc (24 st)
Rnd 6: *3 sc, Inc.* x 6 (30 st)
Rnd 7: SC in each stitch around (30 st)
Rnd 8: 2 sc, Inc., *4 sc, Inc.* x 5, 2 sc (36 st)
Rnd 9: SC in each stitch around (36 st)
Rnd 10: *5 sc, Inc.* x 6 (42 st)
Rnds 11–26: SC in each stitch around (42 st)
Insert the eyes between round 11 and 12 with 7 stitches in between.
Rnd 27: *5 sc, dec.* x 6 (36 st)
Rnd 28: SC in each stitch around (36 st)
Rnd 29: 2 sc, dec., *4 sc, dec.* x 5, 2 sc (30 st)
Start stuffing.

Rnd 30: *3 sc, dec.* x 6 (24 st)
Rnd 31: 1 sc, dec., *2 sc, dec.* x 5, 1 sc (18 st)
Rnd 32: *1 sc, dec.* x 6 (12 st)
Rnd 33: Dec. 6 times (6 st)
Stuff tightly. Cut the yarn and weave it through the remaining 6 stitches using a tapestry needle. Pull tight, and weave it in.

SNOUT

In white

Rnd 1: Start with a magic ring
Rnd 2: 6 sc in MR (6 st)
Rnd 3: *2 Inc., dcinc * x 2 (12 st)
Finish with 1 sl st, cut the yarn leaving enough length for sewing. Embroider the snout with black yarn in the center of the white disk.

EARS

Worked flat, in orange and black.

Rnd 1: (orange) Start with a magic ring
Rnd 2: 6 sc in MR. Do not close. 1 ch, turn (6 st)
Rnd 3: *1 sc, Inc.* x 3 (9 st), 1 sl st. Cut the orange yarn and weave it in
Rnd 4: (black) SC in each stitch around (9 st)
Finish with 1 sl st. Cut the yarn and weave it in.
Make the second ear the same way.

LEGS

In white and orange

Rnd 1: (white) Start with a magic ring
Rnd 2: 6 sc in MR (6 st)
Rnd 3: Inc in all 6 stitches (12 st)

Rnd 4: [BL] (orange) SC in each stitch around (12 st)
Rnd 5: SC in each stitch around (12 st)
Rnd 6: 3 sc, 3 dec., 3 sc (9 st)
Rnds 7–9: SC in each stitch around (9 st)
Rnd 10: *1 sc, dec.* x 3 (6 st)
Stuff tightly. Cut the yarn leaving enough length for sewing, and weave it through the remaining 6 stitches using a tapestry needle, pull tight. Repeat to make the second leg the same way.

ARMS

In white and orange

Rnd 1: (white) Start with a magic ring
Rnd 2: 6 sc in MR (6 st)
Rnd 3: *1 sc, Inc.* x 3 (9 st)
Rnds 4–9: (orange) SC in each stitch around (9 st)
Rnd 10: *1 sc, dec.* x 3 (6 st)
Stuff lightly. Cut the yarn leaving enough length for sewing, and weave it through the remaining 6 stitches using a tapestry needle, pull tight. Repeat to make the second arm the same way.

The ears

The tail

The bowtie

TAIL

In black and orange

Rnd 1: (black) Start with a magic ring
Rnd 2: 6 sc in MR (6 st)
Rnd 3: *1 sc, Inc.* x 3 (9 st)
Rnds 4–6: SC in each stitch around (9 st)
Rnds 7–8: (orange) SC in each stitch around (9 st)
Rnds 9–10: (black) SC in each stitch around (9 st)
Rnds 11–12: (orange) SC in each stitch around (9 st)
Stuff lightly. Finish with 1 sl st, cut the yarn leaving enough length for sewing.

FINISHING

Sew the ears to the head between rows 5 and 11.
Sew the snout to the body between rows 11 and 16.
Sew the arms to the body between rows 16 and 20.
Sew the legs to the body around row 33.
Sew the tail to the back of the body between rows 26 and 29.
Embroider the stripes with a doubled-up strand of black yarn.

BOWTIE

In white

Rnd 1: 18 ch. You'll now be working in the round. The first stitch of Rnd 2 is the first stitch of the chain. Be careful not to twist the chain.
Rnds 2–5: SC in each stitch around (18 st)
Finish with 1 sl st. Flatten the piece and wrap the yarn around the center to shape the bowtie. Secure the yarn and cut it leaving enough length for sewing.
Sew the bowtie under the snout or near one of the ears.

MR. MINI FOX AND MASK

LEVEL: **BEGINNER**

SIZE: 4¼″ (11cm)

MATERIALS

- Hook size D/3 (3mm) or whatever matches your yarn, if using a different kind
- Scheepjes Catona Cotton yarn (100% mercerized cotton) or similar yarn:

    1 skein in rust (main color), approx. 60 yards (60m)

    1 skein in black, approx. 10 yards (10m)

    1 skein in white, approx. 10 yards (10m)

- Two 6mm safety eyes (or black embroidery cotton yarn)
- Stuffing
- Tapestry needle
- Scissors

TECHNIQUES USED

- ch (chain)
- sc (single crochet)
- sl st (slip stitch)
- picot
- inc. (increase)
- dec. (invisible decrease)
- FL / BL (front loop / back loop)
- magic ring (page 8)

NOTES

1 This amigurumi is crocheted in the round, unless specified otherwise.

2 If this stuffed animal is for a child, go down one hook size if you crochet loosely.

3 If this stuffed animal is for an infant, replace the safety eyes with embroidered eyes.

INSTRUCTIONS

HEAD AND BODY

In rust

Rnd 1: Start with a magic ring

Rnd 2: 6 sc in MR (6 st)

Rnd 3: Inc in all 6 sts (12 st)

Rnd 4: *1 sc, Inc.* x 6 (18 st)

Rnd 5: 1 sc, Inc., *2 sc, Inc.* x 5, 1 sc (24 st)

Rnd 6: *3 sc, Inc.* x 6 (30 st)

Rnd 7: SC in each stitch around (30 st)

Rnd 8: 2 sc, Inc., *4 sc, Inc.* x 5, 2 sc (36 st)

Rnd 9: SC in each stitch around (36 st)

Rnd 10: *5 sc, Inc.* x 6 (42 st)

Rnds 11–26: SC in each stitch around (42 st)

Insert the eyes between round 11 and 12 with 7 stitches in between.

Rnd 27: *5 sc, dec.* x 6 (36 st)

Rnd 28: SC in each stitch around (36 st)

Start stuffing

Rnd 29: 2 sc, dec., *4 sc, dec.* x 5, 2 sc (30 st)

Rnd 30: *3 sc, dec.* x 6 (24 st)

Rnd 31: 1 sc, dec., *2 sc, dec.* x 5, 1 sc (18 st)
Rnd 32: *1 sc, dec.* x 6 (12 st)
Rnd 33: Dec. 6 times (6 st)
Stuff tightly. Cut the yarn and weave it through the remaining 6 stitches using a tapestry needle, pull tight and weave it in.

SNOUT

In black, white, and rust

Rnd 1: (black) Start with a magic ring
Rnd 2: 6 sc in MR (6 st)
Rnd 3: SC in each stitch around (6 st)
Rnd 4: (white) *1 sc, Inc.* x 3 (9 st)
Rnd 5: 1 sc, Inc., *2 sc, Inc.* x 2, 1 sc (12 st)
Rnd 6: SC in each stitch around (12 st)
Rnd 7: (orange) *3 sc, Inc.* x 3 (15 st)
Stuff lightly. Finish with 1 sl st, cut the yarn leaving enough length for sewing.

EARS

In black and rust

Rnd 1: (black) Start with a magic ring
Rnd 2: 6 sc in MR (6 st)
Rnd 3: SC in each stitch around (6 st)
Rnd 4: (orange) Inc in all 6 stitches (12 st)
Rnd 5: SC in each stitch around (12 st)
Rnd 6: *1 sc, Inc.* x 6 (18 st)
Rnd 7: SC in each stitch around (18 st)
Finish with 1 sl st, cut the yarn leaving enough length for sewing.
Make the second ear the same way.

ARMS

In black and rust

Rnd 1: (black) Start with a magic ring
Rnd 2: 6 sc in MR (6 st)
Rnd 3: *1 sc, Inc.* x 3 (9 st)
Rnds 4–9: (orange) SC in each stitch around (9 st)
Rnd 10: *1 sc, dec.* x 3 (6 st)
Stuff lightly. Cut the yarn leaving enough length for sewing and weave it through the remaining 6 stitches using a tapestry needle, pull tight.
Make the second arm the same way.

LEGS

In black and rust

Rnd 1: (black) Start with a magic ring
Rnd 2: 6 sc in MR (6 st)
Rnd 3: Inc in all 6 stitches (12 st)
Rnd 4: [BL] (orange) SC in each stitch around (12 st)
Rnd 5: SC in each stitch around (12 st)
Rnd 6: 3 sc, 3 dec., 3 sc (9 st)
Rnds 7–9: SC in each stitch around (9 st)
Rnd 10: *1 sc, dec.* x 3 (6 st)
Stuff tightly. Cut the yarn leaving enough length for sewing and weave it through the remaining 6 stitches using a tapestry needle, pull tight.
Make the second leg the same way.

The snout

The tail

The mask

TAIL

In white and rust

Rnd 1: (white) Start with a magic ring
Rnd 2: 3 sc in MR (3 st)
Rnd 3: Inc in all 3 stitches (6 st)
Rnd 4: *1 sc, Inc.* x 3 (9 st)
Rnd 5: 1 sc, Inc., *2 sc, Inc.* x 2, 1 sc (12 st)
Rnd 6: *3 sc, Inc.* x 3 (15 st)
Rnd 7: SC in each stitch around (15 st)
Rnds 8–10: (orange) SC in each stitch around (15 st)
Rnd 11: *3 sc, dec.* x 3 (12 st)
Rnds 12–13: SC in each stitch around (12 st)
Rnd 14: 1 sc, dec., *2 sc, dec.* x 2, 1sc (9 st)
Rnd 15: SC in each stitch around (9 st) Stuff tightly. Finish with 1 sl st, then cut the yarn leaving enough length for sewing.

FINISHING

Sew the ears to the head between rows 4 and 10.
Sew the snout to the head between rows 11 and 16.
Sew the arms to the body between rows 16 and 20.
Sew the legs to the body around row 33.
Sew the tail to the back of the body between rows 15 and 28.

MASK

Worked flat in black.

Row 1: Start by making a 24-stitch chain, then insert your hook into the 16th stitch from the hook (8th stitch from the beginning of the chain) and make 1 sl st. Then, ch 8 and close the piece by making 1 sl st into the first stitch of the chain. This will create the shape of an 8.

Row 2: 12 sc, skip the center stitch, 24 sc, skip the center stitch, 12 sc (48 st)
Work your sc without inserting into the stitch from row 0 (the chain) but rather by wrapping it (directly in the loop)

Row 3: 11 sc, dec., 11 sc, picot, 11 sc, dec., 11 sc, picot (46 st)
Finish with 1 sl st, then make a 1″ to 1½″ (3–4cm) chain, depending on how loose you crochet. Crochet a 1″ to 1½″ (3–4cm) chain on the other side of the mask as well. Use the two chains to tie the mask on the face.

MS. MINI CHICKEN AND CAPE

LEVEL: INTERMEDIATE

SIZE: 4¼″ (11cm)

MATERIALS

- Hook size D/3 (3mm) or whatever matches your yarn, if using a different kind
- Scheepjes Catona Cotton yarn (100% mercerized cotton) or similar yarn:

    1 skein in yellow (main color), approx. 50 yards (50m)

    1 skein in orange, approx. 10 yards (10m)

    1 skein in red, approx. 30 yards (30m)

- Two 6mm safety eyes (or black embroidery cotton yarn)
- Stuffing
- Tapestry needle
- Scissors

TECHNIQUES USED

- ch (chain)
- sc (single crochet)
- sl st (slip stitch)
- inc. (increase)
- dec. (invisible decrease)
- magic ring (page 8)

NOTES

1 This amigurumi is crocheted in the round, unless specified otherwise.

2 If this stuffed animal is for a child, go down one hook size if you crochet loosely.

3 If this stuffed animal is for an infant, replace the safety eyes with embroidered eyes.

INSTRUCTIONS

HEAD AND BODY

In yellow

Rnd 1: Start with a magic ring
Rnd 2: 6 sc in MR (6 st)
Rnd 3: Inc in all 6 stitches (12 st)
Rnd 4: *1 sc, Inc.* x 6 (18 st)
Rnd 5: 1 sc, Inc., *2 sc, Inc.* x 5, 1 sc (24 st)
Rnd 6: *3 sc, Inc.* x 6 (30 st)
Rnd 7: SC in each stitch around (30 st)
Rnd 8: 2 sc, Inc., *4 sc, Inc.* x 5, 2 sc (36 st)
Rnd 9: SC in each stitch around (36 st)
Rnd 10: *5 sc, Inc.* x 6 (42 st)
Rnds 11–26: SC in each stitch around (42 st)
Insert the eyes between round 10 and 11 with 7 stitches in between.
Rnd 27: *5 sc, dec.* x 6 (36 st)
Rnd 28: SC in each stitch around (36 st)
Start stuffing.
Rnd 29: 2 sc, dec., *4 sc, dec.* x 5, 2 sc (30 st)
Rnd 30: *3 sc, dec.* x 6 (24 st)

The crest

The wings

Rnd 31: 1 sc, dec., *2 sc, dec.* x 5, 1 sc (18 st)
Rnd 32: *1 sc, dec.* x 6 (12 st)
Rnd 33: Dec. 6 times (6 st)
Stuff tightly. Cut the yarn and weave it through the remaining 6 stitches using a tapestry needle, pull tight and weave it in.

CREST

In red
Rnd 1: Start with a magic ring
Rnd 2: 3 sc in MR (3 st)
Rnd 3: * 1 sl st, 5 ch. Starting from the 2nd chain from the hook, sc in the next 4 stitches * repeat for each sc in the MR

Finish with 1 sl st, cut the yarn leaving enough length for sewing.

BEAK

In orange
Rnd 1: Start with a magic ring
Rnd 2: 3 sc in MR (3 st)
Rnd 3: Inc in all 3 stitches (6 st)
Rnd 4: SC in each stitch around (6 st)
Rnd 5: *1 sc, Inc.* x 3 (9 st)
Finish with 1 sl st, cut the yarn leaving enough length for sewing.

WINGS

Worked flat in yellow.
Row 1: 6 ch, turn
Row 2: Inc., 3 sc, Inc., 1 ch, turn (7 st)
Rows 3–4: 7 sc, 1 ch, turn

Row 5: 5 sc, dec., 1 ch, turn (6 st)
Row 6: 6 sc, 1 ch, turn
Row 7: 4 sc, dec., 1 ch, turn (5 st)
Row 8: 5 sc, 1 ch, turn
Row 9: dec., 1 sc, dec., 1 ch, turn (3 st)
Row 10: dec., 1 sc, 1 ch, turn (2 st)
Row 11: dec (1 st)
End with a single crochet edge around the wing for a pretty finish (page 12). Finish with a sl st, cut the yarn and weave it in.
Make the second wing the same way.

FEET

In orange

Start by making three toes, which will be on the end of the feet.

Rnd 1: Start with a magic ring

Rnd 2: 4 sc in MR (4 st)

Finish with 1 sl st, cut the yarn and weave it in for all three toes.

Rnd 3: Place the three toes side by side. You'll now crochet around the three toes to connect them. To do so, crochet 2 stitches from each toe, then continue the round to connect the other 6 stitches on the other side of the toes, as shown in the diagram below.

Rnd 4: SC in each stitch around (12 st)

Rnd 5: Dec. 8 times (6 st)

Rnd 6: *1 sc, dec.* x 2 (4 st)

Rnd 7: SC in each stitch around (4 st)

No need to stuff. Cut the yarn and weave it through the remaining 4 stitches using a tapestry needle, pull tight and weave it in.

Make the second foot the same way.

TAIL

Worked flat in yellow.

Row 1: 5 ch, turn

Rows 2–5: 4 sc, 1 ch, turn (4 st)

Row 6: Dec. 2 times (2 st)

End with a single crochet edge around the tail for a pretty finish (page 12). Finish with a sl st, and cut the yarn, leaving enough length for sewing.

FINISHING

Sew the crest to the top of the head at row 1.

Sew the beak to the head, between rows 12 and 15.

Sew the wings to the body between rows 13 and 22.

Sew the feet to the body around row 33.

Sew the tail to the back of the body at row 25.

CAPE

Worked flat in red.

Row 1: 36 ch

Rows 2–21: 35 sc, 1 ch, turn

Row 22: SC in each stitch (35 st)

Finish with 1 sl st, cut the yarn leaving enough length for sewing. With yellow yarn, embroider the back of the cape with a C or the letter of your choice, in sl st or simple stitching.

Sew the cape on, just above the wings.

The cape

MS. DRAGON AND SURFBOARD

LEVEL: INTERMEDIATE

SIZE: 8˝ (28cm)

MATERIALS

- Hook size D/3 (3mm) or whatever matches your yarn, if using a different kind
- Scheepjes Catona Cotton yarn (100% mercerized cotton) or similar yarn:

  1 skein in blue (main color), approx. 125 yards (125m)

  1 skein in light blue, approx. 25 yards (25m)

  1 skein in yellow, approx. 30 yards (30m)

  1 skein in orange, approx. 10 yards (10m)

- Two 6mm safety eyes (or black embroidery cotton yarn)
- Cardboard (for the bodyboard)
- Stuffing
- Tapestry needle / Scissors

TECHNIQUES USED

- ch (chain)
- sc (single crochet)
- sl st (slip stitch)
- hdc (half double crochet)
- dc (double crochet)
- picot
- inc. (increase)
- dec. (invisible decrease)
- magic ring (page 8)

NOTES

1 This amigurumi is crocheted in the round, unless specified otherwise.

2 If this stuffed animal is for a child, go down one hook size if you crochet loosely.

3 If this stuffed animal is for an infant, replace the safety eyes with embroidered eyes.

4 There are two options for placing the arms: You may sew them at the end, or, for a more secure finish, you may crochet them at the same time as round 30 of the body (page 14).

INSTRUCTIONS

HEAD

In blue

Rnd 1: Start with a magic ring
Rnd 2: 6 sc in MR (6 st)
Rnd 3: Inc in all 6 stitches (12 st)
Rnd 4: *1 sc, Inc.* x 6 (18 st)
Rnd 5: *2 sc, Inc.* x 6 (24 st)
Rnds 6–8: SC in each stitch around (24 st)
Rnd 9: *5 sc, Inc.* x 4 (28 st)
Rnd 10: SC in each stitch around (28 st)
Rnd 11: *6 sc, Inc.* x 4 (32 st)
Rnd 12: SC in each stitch around (32 st)
Rnd 13: *7 sc, Inc.* x 4 (36 st)
Rnds 14–15: SC in each stitch around (36 st)
Rnd 16: *8 sc, Inc.* x 4 (40 st)

The gills

Rnds 17–18: SC in each stitch around (40 st)

Insert the eyes between row 18 and 19 with 14 stitches in between.

Rnd 19: *9 sc, Inc.* x 4 (44 st)

Rnds 20–21: SC in each stitch around (44 st)

Rnd 22: *10 sc, Inc.* x 4 (48 st)

Start stuffing.

Rnds 23–25: SC in each stitch around (48 st)

Rnd 26: 3 sc, dec., *6 sc, dec.* x 5, 3 sc (42 st)

Rnd 27: *5 sc, dec.* x 6 (36 st)

Rnd 28: 2 sc, dec., *4 sc, dec.* x 5, 2 sc (30 st)

Rnd 29: *3 sc, dec.* x 6 (24 st)

Rnd 30: 1 sc, dec., *2 sc, dec.* x 5, 1 sc (18 st)

Rnd 31: *1 sc, dec.* x 6 (12 st)

Rnd 32: Dec. 6 times (6 st)

Stuff tightly. Cut the yarn and weave it through the remaining 6 stitches using a tapestry needle, pull tight and weave it in. Embroider the nostrils with light blue yarn.

GILLS

Worked flat in light blue.

Row 1: 9 ch, turn.

Row 2: Inc., 6 sc, Inc., 1 ch, turn (10 st)

Row 3: Inc., 8 sc, Inc., 1 ch, turn (12 st)

Row 4: 3 sc, 2 hdc, 2 dc, 2 hdc, 3 sc (12 st)

Finish with 1 sl st, then cut the yarn leaving enough length for sewing. Make the second gill the same way.

BODY

In blue

Rnd 1: Start with a magic ring
Rnd 2: 6 sc in MR (6 st)
Rnd 3: Inc. in all 6 stitches (12 st)
Rnd 4: *1 sc, Inc.* x 6 (18 st)
Rnd 5: 1 sc, Inc., *2 sc, Inc.* x 5, 1 sc (24 st)
Rnd 6: *3 sc, Inc.* x 6 (30 st)
Rnd 7: 2 sc, Inc., *4 sc, Inc.* x 5, 2 sc (36 st)
Rnd 8: *5 sc, Inc.* x 6 (42 st)
Rnd 9: 3 sc, Inc., *6 sc, Inc.* x 5, 3 sc (48 st)
Rnd 10: *7 sc, Inc.* x 6 (54 st)
Rnd 11: 4 sc, Inc., *8 sc, Inc.* x 5, 4 sc (60 st)
Rnds 12–16: SC in each stitch around (60 st)
Rnd 17: 4 sc, dec., *8 sc, dec.* x 5, 4 sc (54 st)
Rnds 18–19: SC in each stitch around (54 st)
Rnd 20: *7 sc, dec.* x 6 (48 st)
Rnds 21–22: SC in each stitch around (48 st)
Rnd 23: 3 sc, dec., *6 sc, dec.* x 5, 3 sc (42 st)
Start stuffing
Rnds 24–25: SC in each stitch around (42 st)
Rnd 26: *5 sc, dec.* x 6 (36 st)
Rnds 27–29: SC in each stitch around (36 st)
Rnd 30: 2 sc, dec., *4 sc, dec.* x 5, 2 sc (30 st)
Attach arms (page 14)
Rnds 31–33: SC in each stitch around (30 st)
Stuff tightly. Finish with 1 sl st. Cut the yarn leaving enough length for sewing.

ARMS

In blue

Rnd 1: Start with a magic ring
Rnd 2: 6 sc in MR (6 st)
Rnd 3: *1 sc, Inc.* x 3 (9 st)
Rnds 4–11: SC in each stitch around (9 st)
No stuffing necessary. Finish with 1 sl st and cut the yarn. Don't forget to leave enough length to attach it at the end if you prefer to sew. Otherwise, weave the yarn in.
Crochet the claws with your secondary color (light blue). Flatten the arm and crochet along the first rows in the following pattern: 1 sl st, *picot, 1 sl st* x 3.
Make the second arm the same way.

The arms

The body

LEGS

In blue

Rnd 1: Start with a magic ring
Rnd 2: 6 sc in MR (6 st)
Rnd 3: Inc. in all 6 stitches (12 st)
Rnds 4–9: SC in each stitch around (12 st)
Rnd 10: 6 dec. (6 st)
Stuff lightly. Cut the yarn, leaving enough length for sewing, and weave it through the remaining 6 stitches using a tapestry needle. Pull tight. Crochet the claws with your secondary color (light blue). Flatten the foot and crochet along the first rows in the following pattern: 1 sl st, *picot, 1 sl st* x 3.
Make the second leg the same way.

FLIPPERS

In light blue

Row 1: 13 ch, turn
Rnd 2: 11 sc, 3 sc in the 12th stitch (last stitch). Do not turn. Continue working along the chain to create an oval: 10 sc, 2 sc in the last stitch (the very first one you worked) (26 st). Starting now you'll be working in the round.
Rnds 3–8: Inc., 10 sc, 2 dec., 10 sc, Inc. (26 st)
Finish with 1 sl st. Cut the yarn, leaving enough length for sewing.
Make the second flipper the same way.

TAIL

In blue

Rnd 1: Start with a magic ring
Rnd 2: 6 sc in MR (6 st)
Rnds 3–4: SC in each stitch around (6 st)
Rnd 5: *1 sc, Inc.* x 3 (9 st)
Rnds 6–7: SC in each stitch around (9 st)
Rnd 8: 1 sc, Inc., *2 sc, Inc.* x 2, 1 sc (12 st)
Rnds 9–11: SC in each stitch around (12 st)
Rnd 12: 5 sc, 2 Inc, 5 sc (14 st)
Start stuffing
Rnd 13: SC in each stitch around (14 st)
Rnd 14: 6 sc, 2 Inc., 6 sc (16 st)
Rnd 15: SC in each stitch around (16 st)
Rnd 16: 6 sc, 2 Inc., 6 sc (16 st)
Rnd 17: SC in each stitch around (18 st)
Rnd 18: 8 sc, 2 Inc., 8 sc (20 st)
Rnd 19: SC in each stitch around (20 st)

The legs & claws

The flippers

Rnd 20: 9 sc, 2 Inc., 9 sc (22 st)
Rnd 21: 10 sc, 2 Inc., 10 sc (24 st)
Rnd 22: 11 sc, 2 Inc., 11 sc (26 st)
Rnd 23: 12 sc, 2 Inc., 12 sc (28 st)
Rnd 24: 13 sc, 2 Inc., 13 sc (30 st)
Stuff tightly. Finish with 1 sl st. Cut the yarn leaving enough length for sewing.

FINS (FOR THE TAIL)

In light blue

Row 1: 6 ch, turn
Rnd 2: 4 sc, 3 sc in the 5th stitch (the last stitch). Do not turn. Continue working along the chain to create an oval: 3 sc, 2 sc in the last stitch (the very first one you worked) (12 st). You'll now be working in the round.
Rnds 3–4: Inc., 3 sc, 2 dec., 3 sc, Inc. (12 st)
Finish with 1 sl st. Cut the yarn leaving enough length for sewing.
Make the other 2 fins the same way.

The fin

FINISHING

Sew the gills to the head. They should be placed on row 25.
Attach the head to the body. You should have left enough yarn when finishing the body to sew it to the head. Simply place the head on the opening of the body, finish stuffing tightly, then sew them together.
Sew the arms to the body if you haven't attached them while crocheting the body. They should be placed around row 30.
Sew the legs to the body. They should be placed at the base of the body around row 7.
Sew the flippers to the body. They should be placed between rows 20 and 33, with 1 stitch in between at the top and 7 stitches in between at the bottom.
Sew the fins to the tail. They should be placed between rows 3 and 8, two horizontally and one vertically.
Sew the tail to the body. It should be placed between rows 9 and 20.

SURFBOARD

In yellow and orange

Row 1: (yellow) 9 ch, turn
Rnd 2: 7 sc, 3 sc in the 8th st (the last stitch). Do not turn. Continue working along the chain to create an oval: 6 sc, 2 sc in the last stitch (the very first one you worked) (18 st). Starting now you'll be working in the round.
Rnd 3: *8 sc, Inc.* x 2 (20 st)
Rnd 4: *9 sc, Inc.* x 2 (22 st)
Rnd 5: *10 sc, Inc.* x 2 (24 st)
Rnd 6: *11 sc, Inc.* x 2 (26 st)
Rnd 7: *12 sc, Inc.* x 2 (28 st)
Rnd 8: *13 sc, Inc.* x 2 (30 st)
Rnd 9: *14 sc, Inc.* x 2 (32 st)
Rnd 10: *15 sc, Inc.* x 2 (34 st)
Rnd 11: SC in each stitch around (34 st)
Rnds 12–14: (orange) SC in each stitch around (34 st)
Rnds 15–23: (yellow) SC in each stitch around (34 st)
Rnd 24: 14 sc, 1 hdc, {3 dc}, 1 hdc, 14 sc, 1 hdc, {3 dc}, 1 hdc, 1 sl st
Do not cut the yarn. Draw the outline of the surfboard on a piece of cardboard, cut it and insert it inside your piece. Close the surfboard, either by sewing it shut or by crocheting into two stitches simultaneously (page 12).

MR. UNICORN AND CLOUD

LEVEL: **INTERMEDIATE**

SIZE: **8″ (20cm)**

MATERIALS

- Hook size D/3 (3mm) or whatever matches your yarn, if using a different kind
- Scheepjes Catona Cotton yarn (100% mercerized cotton) or similar yarn:

  1 skein in white (main color), approx. 125 yards (125m)

  1 skein in yellow, approx. 15 yards (15m)

  1 skein in light blue, approx. 20 yards (20m)

  For each color of the rainbow, approx. 15 yards (15m)

- Two 6mm safety eyes (or black embroidery cotton yarn)
- Stuffing
- Tapestry needle
- Scissors

TECHNIQUES USED

- ch (chain)
- sc (single crochet)
- sl st (slip stitch)
- inc. (increase)
- dec. (invisible decrease)
- magic ring (page 8)
- FL / BL (front loop / back loop)

NOTES

1 This amigurumi is crocheted in the round, unless specified otherwise.

2 If this stuffed animal is for a child, go down one hook size if you crochet loosely.

3 If this stuffed animal is for an infant, replace the safety eyes with embroidered eyes.

4 There are two options for placing the arms: You may sew them at the end, or, for a more secure finish, you may crochet them at the same time as round 30 of the body (page 14).

INSTRUCTIONS

HEAD

In white

Rnd 1: Start with a magic ring

Rnd 2: 6 sc in MR (6 st)

Rnd 3: Inc. in all 6 stitches (12 st)

Rnd 4: *1 sc, Inc.* x 6 (18 st)

Rnd 5: SC in each stitch around (18 st)

Rnd 6: *5 sc, Inc.* x 3 (21 st)

Rnds 7–8: SC in each stitch around (21 st)

Rnd 9: *6 sc, Inc.* x 3 (24 st)

Rnd 10: SC in each stitch around (24 st)

Rnd 11: *7 sc, Inc.* x 3 (27 st)

Rnd 12: SC in each stitch around (27 st)

Rnd 13: *8 sc, Inc.* x 3 (30 st)

Rnd 14: SC in each stitch around (30 st)

Rnd 15: 2 sc, Inc., *4 sc, Inc.* x 5, 2 sc (36 st)

Rnd 16: SC in each stitch around (36 st)

Rnd 17: *5 sc, Inc.* x 6 (42 st)
Insert eyes between row 17 and 18 (with 14 stitches in between).
Rnd 18: SC in each stitch around (42 st)
Rnd 19: 3 sc, Inc., *6 sc, Inc.* x 5, 3 sc (48 st)
Rnds 20–23: SC in each stitch around (48 st)
Rnd 24: 3 sc, dec., *6 sc, dec.* x 5, 3 sc (42 st)
Start stuffing.
Rnd 25: *5 sc, dec.* x 6 (36 st)
Rnd 26: 2 sc, dec., *4 sc, dec.* x 5, 2 sc (30 st)
Rnd 27: *3 sc, dec.* x 6 (24 st)
Rnd 28: 1 sc, dec., *2 sc, dec.* x 5, 1 sc (18 st)
Rnd 29: *1 sc, dec.* x 6 (12 st)
Rnd 30: Dec. 6 times (6 st)
Stuff tightly. Cut the yarn and weave it through the remaining 6 stitches using a tapestry needle, pull tight and weave it in. Embroider the nostrils with yellow yarn.

EARS

In white
Rnd 1: Start with a magic ring
Rnd 2: 4 sc in MR (4 st)
Rnd 3: SC in each stitch around (4 st)
Rnd 4: Inc. in all 4 stitches (8 st)
Rnd 5: SC in each stitch around (8 st)
Rnd 6: *1 sc, Inc.* x 4 (12 st)
Rnds 7–10: SC in each stitch around (12 st)
Rnd 11: *1 sc, dec.* x 4 (8 st)
No need to stuff. Finish with 1 sl st. Cut the yarn leaving enough length for sewing.
Make the second ear the same way.

HORN

In yellow
Row 1: 9 ch
Starting now, you'll be working in the round (be careful not to twist the chain); the first stitch of round 1 is the first stitch of the chain (row 1).
Rnds 2–4: [BL] SC in each stitch around (9 st)
Rnd 5: [BL] *1 sc, dec.* x 3 (6 st)
Rnds 6–7: [BL] SC in each stitch around (6 st)
Rnd 8: [BL] Dec. 3 times (3 st)
Stuff tightly. Cut the yarn and weave it through the remaining 3 stitches using a tapestry needle, pull tight and weave it in.

The horn

The ears

BODY

In white

Rnd 1: Start with a magic ring
Rnd 2: 6 sc in MR (6 st)
Rnd 3: Inc. in all 6 stitches (12 st)
Rnd 4: *1 sc, Inc.* x 6 (18 st)
Rnd 5: 1 sc, Inc., *2 sc, Inc.* x 5, 1 sc (24 st)
Rnd 6: *3 sc, Inc.* x 6 (30 st)
Rnd 7: 2 sc, Inc., *4 sc, Inc.* x 5, 2 sc (36 st)
Rnd 8: *5 sc, Inc.* x 6 (42 st)
Rnd 9: 3 sc, Inc., *6 sc, Inc.* x 5, 3 sc (48 st)
Rnd 10: *7 sc, Inc.* x 6 (54 st)
Rnd 11: 4 sc, Inc., *8 sc, Inc.* x 5, 4 sc (60 st)
Rnds 12–16: SC in each stitch around (60 st)
Rnd 17: 4 sc, dec., *8 sc, dec.* x 5, 4 sc (54 st)
Rnds 18–19: SC in each stitch around (54 st)
Rnd 20: *7 sc, dec.* x 6 (48 st)
Rnds 21–22: SC in each stitch around (48 st)
Rnd 23: 3 sc, dec., *6 sc, dec.* x 5, 3 sc (42 st)
Start stuffing.
Rnds 24–25: SC in each stitch around (42 st)
Rnd 26: *5 sc, dec.* x 6 (36 st)
Rnds 27–29: SC in each stitch around (36 st)
Rnd 30: 2 sc, dec., *4 sc, dec.* x 5, 2 sc (30 st)
Attach the arms (page 14).
Rnds 31–33: SC in each stitch around (30 st)
Stuff tightly. Finish with 1 sl st. Cut the yarn, leaving enough length for sewing.

ARMS

In white

Rnd 1: (yellow) Start with a magic ring
Rnd 2: 6 sc in MR (6 st)
Rnd 3: Inc. in all 6 stitches (12 st)
Rnd 4: [BL] SC in each stitch around (12 st)
Rnd 5: 4 sc, 2 dec., 4 sc (10 st)
Rnd 6: (white) SC in each stitch around (10 st)
Rnd 7: 4 sc, dec., 4 sc (9 st)
Rnds 8–11: SC in each stitch around (9 st)
Stuff the hoof lightly. Finish with 1 sl st. If you prefer to sew the arm at the end then cut the yarn leaving enough length to do so, otherwise weave it in. Make the second arm the same way.

The arms

The body

The legs

The mane

LEGS

In white and yellow

Rnd 1: (yellow) Start with a magic ring

Rnd 2: 6 sc in MR (6 st)

Rnd 3: Inc. in all 6 stitches (12 st)

Rnd 4: *1 sc, Inc.* x 6 (18 st)

Rnd 5: [BL] SC in each stitch around (18 st)

Rnd 6: 6 sc, 3 dec., 6 sc (15 st)

Rnd 7: (white) SC in each stitch around (15 st)

Rnd 8: 5 sc, 3 dec., 4 sc (12 st)

Rnds 9–11: SC in each stitch around (12 st)

Rnd 12: Dec. 6 times (6 st)

Stuff tightly. Cut the yarn leaving enough length for sewing and weave it through the remaining 6 stitches using a tapestry needle, pull tight and weave it in.

Make the second leg the same way.

MANE

In rainbow colors (use all the colors you'd like).

Start by making a 30-st chain. Insert your hook between 2 stitches on the head and make a slip stitch to attach it. Make 29 slip stitches along the chain (page 16).

Cut the yarn and weave it in.

Make as many strands as you'd like, in any color you want. Ideally, they should run from right behind where the horn will be, to where the ears will be.

Attach the head to the body. You should have left enough yarn when finishing the body to sew it to the head. Simply place the head on the opening of the body and finish stuffing tightly, then sew them together.

Sew the arms to the body if you haven't attached them while crocheting the body. They should be placed around row 30.

Sew the legs to the body. They should be placed at the base of the body, around row 6.

TAIL

In rainbow colors (use all the colors you'd like).

In rainbow colors (use all the colors you'd like).

Start by making a 16-st chain. Insert your hook between 2 stitches at the base of the body and make a slip stitch to attach it. Make 15 slip stitches along the chain (page 16). Cut the yarn and weave it in.

The best place for those strands is between rows 7 and 9, on the back of the body.

FINISHING

Sew the horn to the head between the eyes and between rows 18 and 20. Sew the ears to the head at row 24.

CLOUD

In blue

Rnd 1: Start with a magic ring

Rnd 2: 6 sc in MR (6 st)

Rnd 3: Inc. in all 6 stitches (12 st)

Rnd 4: *1 sc, Inc.* x 6 (18 st)

Rnd 5: SC in each stitch around (18 st)

Rnd 6: 7 sc, 2 dec., 7 sc (16 st)

Rnd 7: 7 sc, 2 Inc., 7 sc (18 st)

Rnd 8: 8 sc, 2 Inc., 8 sc (20 st)

Rnd 9: 9 sc, 2 Inc., 9 sc (22 st)

Rnd 10: SC in each stitch around (22 st)

Rnd 11: 9 sc, 2 dec., 9 sc (20 st)

Rnd 12: 8 sc, 2 dec., 8 sc (18 st)

Rnd 13: 8 sc, 2 Inc., 8 sc (20 st)

Rnd 14: 9 sc, 2 Inc., 9 sc (22 st)

Rnd 15: 10 sc, 2 Inc., 10 sc (24 st)

Rnd 16: 11 sc, 2 Inc., 11 sc (26 st)

Rnd 17: SC in each stitch around (26 st)

Rnd 18: 11 sc, 2 dec., 11 sc (24 st)

Rnd 19: 10 sc, 2 dec., 10 sc (22 st)

Rnd 20: 9 sc, 2 dec., 9 sc (20 st)

Rnd 21: 8 sc, 2 dec., 8 sc (18 st)

Rnd 22: 7 sc, 2 dec., 7 sc (16 st)

Rnd 23: 7 sc, 2 Inc., 7 sc (18 st)

Rnd 24: *1 sc, dec.* x 6 (12 st)

Rnd 25: Dec. 6 times (6 st)

Stuff tightly. Cut the yarn and weave it through the remaining 6 stitches using a tapestry needle, pull tight and weave it in. Embroider the face with black yarn.

For the cheeks, make a magic ring with 6 sc, cut the yarn, and sl st the first stitch of the ring to close it. Now simply sew it to the cloud.

The Tail

The cloud

MS. MINI OWL AND WITCH HAT

LEVEL: **INTERMEDIATE**

SIZE: 4¼″ (11cm)

MATERIALS

• Hook size D/3 (3mm) or whatever matches your yarn, if using a different kind

• Scheepjes Catona Cotton yarn (100% mercerized cotton) or similar yarn:

    1 skein in beige (main color), approx. 50 yards (50m)

    1 skein in brown, approx. 30 yards (30m)

    1 skein in copper, approx. 20 yards (20m)

• 1 skein in white, approx. 5 yards (5m)

• Two 6mm safety eyes (or black embroidery cotton yarn)

• Stuffing

• Tapestry needle

• Scissors

TECHNIQUES USED

• ch (chain)

• sc (single crochet)

• sl st (slip stitch)

• inc. (increase)

• dec. (invisible decrease)

• magic ring (page 8)

NOTES

1 This amigurumi is crocheted in the round, unless specified otherwise.

2 If this stuffed animal is for a child, go down one hook size if you crochet loosely.

3 If this stuffed animal is for an infant, replace the safety eyes with embroidered eyes.

INSTRUCTIONS

EYES

In white

Rnd 1: Start with a magic ring

Rnd 2: 6 sc in MR (6 st)

Rnd 3: Inc. in all 6 stitches (12 st)

Rnd 4: *1 sc, Inc.* x 6 (18 st)

Finish with 1 sl st, then cut the yarn leaving enough length for sewing. Make the second eye the same way.

HEAD AND BODY

In beige

Rnd 1: Start with a magic ring
Rnd 2: 6 sc in MR (6 st)
Rnd 3: Inc. in all 6 stitches (12 st)
Rnd 4: *1 sc, Inc.* x 6 (18 st)
Rnd 5: 1 sc, Inc., *2 sc, Inc.* x 5, 1 sc (24 st)
Rnd 6: *3 sc, Inc.* x 6 (30 st)
Rnd 7: SC in each stitch around (30 st)
Rnd 8: 2 sc, Inc., *4 sc, Inc.* x 5, 2 sc (36 st)
Rnd 9: SC in each stitch around (36 st)
Rnd 10: *5 sc, Inc.* x 6 (42 st)
Insert the eyes between rows 10 and 11, in the center of the white circles you've already made. There should be one stitch between the circles.
Rnds 11–26: SC in each stitch around (42 st)
Start stuffing.
Rnd 27: *5 sc, dec.* x 6 (36 st)
Rnd 28: SC in each stitch around (36 st)
Rnd 29: 2 sc, dec., *4 sc, dec.* x 5, 2 sc (30 st)

Rnd 30: *3 sc, dec.* x 6 (24 st)
Rnd 31: 1 sc, dec., *2 sc, dec.* x 5, 1 sc (18 st)
Rnd 32: *1 sc, dec.* x 6 (12 st)
Rnd 33: Dec. 6 times (6 st)
Stuff tightly. Cut the yarn and weave it through the remaining 6 stitches using a tapestry needle, pull tight and weave it in. Embroider the beak between rows 13 and 15.

EARS

In brown

Rnd 1: Start with a magic ring
Rnd 2: 4 sc in MR (4 st)
Rnd 3: SC in each stitch around (4 st)
Rnd 4: Inc. in all 4 stitches (8 st)
Rnd 5: SC in each stitch around (8 st)
Rnd 6: *1 sc, Inc.* x 4 (12 st)
No need to stuff. Finish with 1 sl st and cut the yarn, leaving enough length for sewing.
Make the second ear the same way.

WINGS

Worked flat in brown.

Row 1: 6 ch, turn
Row 2: 5 sc, 1 ch, turn (5 st)
Row 3: Inc., 3 sc, Inc., 1 ch, turn (7 st)
Row 4: 7 sc, 1 ch, turn
Row 5: Inc., 5 sc, Inc., 1 ch, turn (9 st)
Rows 6–10: 9 sc, 1 ch, turn
Row 11: dec., 7 sc, 1 ch, turn (8 st)
Row 12: 6 sc, dec., 1 ch, turn (7 st)
Row 13: dec., 5 sc, 1 ch, turn (6 st)
Row 14: dec., 4 sc, 1 ch, turn (5 st)
Row 15: 5 sc, 1 ch, turn
Row 16: dec., 1 sc, dec., 1 ch, turn (3 st)
Row 17–18: 3 sc, 1 ch, turn
Row 19: dec., 1 sc, 1 ch, turn (2 st)
Row 20: dec., 1 ch, turn (1 st)
Row 21: 1 SC
End with a single crochet edge around the wing for a pretty finish (page 12). Finish with a sl st, cut the yarn and weave it in.
Make the second wing the same way.
Reminder: Flip the second wing over before making the finishing edge.

The ears

FEET

In brown

Start by making three toes, which will be on the end of the feet.

Rnd 1: Start with a magic ring

Rnd 2: 4 sc in MR (4 st)

Finish with 1 sl st, cut the yarn and weave it in for all three toes.

Rnd 3: Place the three toes side by side. You'll now crochet around the three toes to connect them. To do so, crochet 2 stitches from each toe, then continue the round to connect the other 6 stitches on the other side of the toes, as shown in the diagram below.

Rnd 4: SC in each stitch around (12 st)

Rnd 5: Dec. 6 times (6 st)

Rnd 6: *1 sc, dec.* x 2 (4 st)

Rnd 7: SC in each stitch around (4 st)
No need to stuff.
Cut the yarn and weave it through the remaining 4 stitches, pull tight and weave it in.
Make the second foot the same way.

TAIL

In brown

Row 1: 8 ch, turn

Rnd 2: 6 sc, 3 sc in the 7th st (the last stitch). Do not turn. Continue working along the chain to create an oval: 5 sc, 2 sc in the last stitch (the very first one you worked) (16 st). You'll now be working in the round.

Rnds 3–7: SC in each stitch around (16 st)

Rnd 8: *6 sc, dec.* x 2 (14 st)

Rnds 9–10: SC in each stitch around (14 st)

Stuff tightly. Finish with 1 sl st and cut the yarn, leaving enough length for sewing.

FINISHING

Sew the ears to the head. Fold them in half at the base to make them concave, and sew them between rows 4 and 8.

Sew the white eye circles to the head. Sew the wings to the body below row 14.

Sew the feet to the body around row 33. Sew the tail to the body between rows 24 and 27.

HAT

In copper

Rnd 1: Start with a magic ring

Rnd 2: 3 sc in MR (3 st)

Rnd 3: SC in each stitch around (3 st)

Rnds 4–5: Inc. in all 3 stitches (6 st)

Rnd 6: SC in each stitch around (6 st)

Rnd 7: *1 sc, Inc.* x 3 (9 st)

Rnd 8: SC in each stitch around (9 st)

Rnd 9: 1 sc, Inc., *2 sc, Inc.* x 2, 1 sc (12 st)

Rnd 10: SC in each stitch around (12 st)

Rnd 11: *3 sc, Inc.* x 3 (15 st)

Rnd 12: SC in each stitch around (15 st)

Rnd 13: 2 sc, Inc., *4 sc, Inc.* x 2, 2 sc (18 st)

Rnd 14: SC in each stitch around (18 st)

Rnd 15: *5 sc, Inc.* x 3 (21 st)

Rnd 16: 3 sc, Inc., *6 sc, Inc.* x 2, 3 sc (24 st)

Rnd 17: *7 sc, Inc.* x 3 (27 st)

Rnd 18: 4 sc, Inc., *8 sc, Inc.* x 2, 4 sc (30 st)

Rnd 19: *9 sc, Inc.* x 3 (33 st)

Rnd 20: 5 sc, Inc., *10 sc, Inc.* x 2, 5 sc (36 st)

Finish with 1 sl st, cut the yarn and weave it in.

The eyes

MS. REINDEER AND SCARF

LEVEL: INTERMEDIATE

SIZE: 8″ (20cm)

MATERIALS

- Hook size D/3 (3mm) or whatever matches your yarn, if using a different kind
- Scheepjes Catona Cotton yarn (100% mercerized cotton) or similar yarn:

    1 skein in light brown, approx. 110 yards (110m)

    1 skein in dark brown, approx. 30 yards (30m)

    1 skein in cream, approx. 10 yards (10m)

    1 skein in red, approx. 20 yards (20m)

- Two 6mm safety eyes (or black embroidery cotton yarn)
- Stuffing
- Tapestry needle
- Scissors

TECHNIQUES USED

- ch (chain)
- sc (single crochet)
- sl st (slip stitch)
- inc. (increase)
- dec. (invisible decrease)
- FL / BL (front loop / back loop)

NOTES

1 This amigurumi is crocheted in the round, unless specified otherwise.

2 If this stuffed animal is for a child, go down one hook size if you crochet loosely.

3 If this stuffed animal is for an infant, replace the safety eyes with embroidered eyes.

4 There are two options for placing the arms: You may sew them at the end, or, for a more secure finish, you may crochet them at the same time as round 30 of the body (page 14).

INSTRUCTIONS

HEAD

In light brown and cream

Rnd 1: (cream) Start with a magic ring

Rnd 2: 6 sc in MR (6 st)

Rnd 3: Inc. in all 6 stiches (12 st)

Rnd 4: *1 sc, Inc.* x 6 (18 st)

Rnd 5: 1 sc, Inc., *2 sc, Inc.* x 5, 1 sc (24 st)

Rnds 6–8: SC in each stitch around (24 st)

Rnd 9: (light brown) SC in each stitch around (24 st)

Rnd 10: *3 sc, Inc.* x 6 (30 st)

Rnds 11–13: SC in each stitch around (30 st)

Rnd 14: 2 sc, Inc., *4 sc, Inc.* x 5, 2 sc (36 st)

Rnd 15: SC in each stitch around (36 st)

Rnd 16: *5 sc, Inc.* x 6 (42 st)

Rnd 17: 3 sc, Inc., *6 sc, Inc.* x 5, 3 sc (48 st)

Rnd 18: SC in each stitch around (48 st)

Insert the eyes between row 18 and 19 (with 15 st in between).

The ears

The back of the antlers

Rnd 19: *7 sc, Inc.* x 6 (54 st)
Rnds 20–22: SC in each stitch around (54 st)
Rnd 23: *7 sc, dec.* x 6 (48 st)
Rnd 24: 3 sc, dec., *6 sc, dec.* x 5, 3 sc (42 st)
Rnd 25: *5 sc, dec.* x 6 (36 st)
Start stuffing.
Rnd 26: 2 sc, dec., *4 sc, dec.* x 5, 2 sc (30 st)
Rnd 27: *3 sc, dec.* x 6 (24 st)
Rnd 28: 1 sc, dec., *2 sc, dec.* x 5, 1 sc (18 st)
Rnd 29: *1 sc, dec.* x 6 (12 st)
Rnd 30: Dec. 6 times (6 st)
Stuff tightly. Cut the yarn and weave it through the remaining 6 stitches using a tapestry needle, pull tight and weave it in.

EARS

In light brown
Rnd 1: Start with a magic ring
Rnd 2: 4 sc in MR (4 st)
Rnd 3: SC in each stitch around (4 st)
Rnd 4: Inc. in all 4 stitches (8 st)
Rnd 5: SC in each stitch around (8 st)
Rnd 6: *1 sc, Inc.* x 4 (12 st)
Rnd 7: 1 sc, Inc., *2 sc, Inc.* x 3, 1 sc (16 st)
Rnds 8–10: SC in each stitch around (16 st)
Rnd 11: 1 sc, dec., *2 sc, dec.* x 3, 1 sc (12 st)
Finish with 1 sl st, then cut the yarn leaving enough length for sewing.
Repeat to make the second ear.

ANTLERS

Worked in three parts.
In dark brown
Part One:
Rnd 1: Start with a magic ring
Rnd 2: 6 sc in MR (6 st)

Rnds 3–12: SC in each stitch around (6 st)
Finish with 1 sl st, then cut the yarn, leaving enough length for sewing.
Part Two:
Rnd 1: Start with a magic ring
Rnd 2: 6 sc in MR (6 st)
Rnds 3–8: SC in each stitch around (6 st)
Finish with 1 sl st, then cut the yarn, leaving enough length for sewing.
Part Three:
Rnd 1: Start with a magic ring
Rnd 2: 6 sc in MR
Rnds 3–5: SC in each stitch around (6 st)
Finish with 1 sl st, then cut the yarn, leaving enough length for sewing.
Lightly stuff all 3 parts. Sew the small piece to the top of the tall piece, and sew the medium piece about halfway along the tall piece.
Repeat to make the second antler.

NOSE

In dark brown

Rnd 1: Start with a magic ring
Rnd 2: 6 sc in MR (6 st)
Rnd 3: Inc. in all 6 stitches (12 st)
Rnd 4: SC in each stitch around (12 st)
Finish with 1 sl st, then cut the yarn leaving enough length for sewing.

ARMS AND HOOFS

In dark and light brown

Rnd 1: (dark brown) Start with a magic ring
Rnd 2: 6 sc in MR (6 st)
Rnd 3: Inc. in all 6 stitches (12 st)
Rnd 4: [BL] SC in each stitch around (12 st)
Rnd 5: 4 sc, 2 dec., 4 sc (10 st)
Rnd 6: (light brown) SC in each stitch around (10 st)
Rnd 7: 4 sc, dec., 4 sc (9 st)

Rnds 8–11: SC in each stitch around (9 st)
Lightly stuff the hoof. Finish with 1 sl st, then cut the yarn leaving enough length for sewing if you wish to do so, otherwise weave it in. Bring a strand of yarn to the middle of the hoof between rows 2 and 5 and pull it tight to create a crease.
Repeat to make the second arm and hoof.

BODY

In light brown

Rnd 1: Start with a magic ring
Rnd 2: 6 sc in MR (6 st)
Rnd 3: Inc. in all 6 stitches (12 st)
Rnd 4: *1 sc, Inc.* x 6 (18 st)
Rnd 5: 1 sc, Inc, *2 sc, Inc.* x 5, 1 sc (24 st)
Rnd 6: *3 sc, Inc.* x 6 (30 st)
Rnd 7: 2 sc, Inc, *4 sc, Inc.* x 5, 2 sc (36 st)
Rnd 8: *5 sc, Inc.* x 6 (42 st)
Rnd 9: 3 sc, Inc, *6 sc, Inc.* x 5, 3 sc (48 st)
Rnd 10: *7 sc, Inc.* x 6 (54 st)
Rnd 11: 4 sc, Inc., *8 sc, Inc.* x 5, 4 sc (60 st)

Rnds 12–16: SC in each stitch around (60 st)
Start stuffing.
Rnd 17: 4 sc, dec., *8 sc, dec.* x 5, 4 sc (54 st)
Rnds 18–19: SC in each stitch around (54 st)
Rnd 20: *7 sc, dec.* x 6 (48 st)
Rnds 21–22: SC in each stitch around (48 st)
Rnd 23: 3 sc, dec., *6 sc, dec.* x 5, 3 sc (42 st)
Rnds 24–25: SC in each stitch around (42 st)
Rnd 26: *5 sc, dec.* x 6 (36 st)
Rnds 27–29: SC in each stitch around (36 st)
Rnd 30: 2 sc, dec., *4 sc, dec.* x 5, 2 sc (30 st)
Attach the arms (page 14).
Rnds 31–33: SC in each stitch around (30 st)
Stuff tightly. Finish with 1 sl st then cut the yarn leaving enough length for sewing.

The nose

The body

The legs

The Tail

LEGS AND HOOFS

In dark and light brown

Rnd 1: (dark brown) Start with a magic ring

Rnd 2: 6 sc in MR (6 st)

Rnd 3: Inc. in all 6 stitches (12 st)

Rnd 4: *1 sc, Inc.* x 6 (18 st)

Rnd 5: [BL] SC in each stitch around (18 st)

Rnd 6: 6 sc, 3 dec., 6 sc (15 st)
Start stuffing.

Rnd 7: (light brown) SC in each stitch around (15 st)

Rnd 8: 5 sc, 3 dec., 4 sc (12 st)

Rnds 9–11: SC in each stitch around (12 st)

Rnd 12: Dec. 6 times (6 st)
Stuff lightly. Finish with 1 sl st then cut the yarn leaving enough length for sewing. Bring a strand of yarn to the middle of the hoof between rows 3 and 6 and pull it tight to create a crease.
Repeat to make the second leg and hoof.

TAIL

In cream

Row 1: 6 ch, turn.

Rnd 2: 4 sc, 3 sc in the 5th stitch (the last stitch). Do not turn. Continue working along the chain to create an oval: 3 sc, 2 sc in the last stitch (the very first one you worked) (12 st). Starting now you'll be working in the round.

Rnd 3: *3 sc, 3 Inc.* x 2 (18 st)

Rnds 4–5: SC in each stitch around (18 st)
Stuff tightly. Finish with 1 sl st then cut the yarn leaving enough length for sewing.

FINISHING

Attach the head to the body. You should have left enough yarn when finishing the body to sew it to the head. Simply place the head on the opening of the body and finish stuffing tightly, then sew them together. Sew the nose to the head between rows 2 and 5.
Sew the ears and antlers to the head. They should all be sewn on row 22.

When sewing the ears, fold them in half to make them hollow at the base. If you haven't attached the arms while crocheting the body, sew them now on row 30.
Sew the legs to the body around row 4.
Sew the tail to the body between rows 8 and 14.

SCARF
Worked flat in red.
Row 1: 3 ch, turn.
Row 2: 2 sc, 1 ch, turn (2 st)
Row 3: 2 Inc., 1 ch, turn (4 st)
Row 4: 4 sc, 1 ch, turn (4 st)
Row 5: Inc., 2 sc, Inc., 1 ch, turn (6 st)
Row 6: 6 sc, 1 ch, turn.
Keep crocheting the scarf until it measures 23½" (60cm).
Next row: dec., 2 sc, dec., 1 ch, turn (4 st)
Next row: 4 sc, 1 ch, turn (4 st)
Next row: 2 dec., 1 ch, turn (2 st)
Next row: 2 sc (2 st)
Fasten off, weave in ends.

The ears and the antlers

The scarf

MS. MINI FROG AND CROWN

LEVEL: **INTERMEDIATE**

SIZE: **4¾˝ (12cm)**

MATERIALS

- Hook size D/3 (3mm) or whatever matches your yarn, if using a different kind
- Scheepjes Catona Cotton yarn (100% mercerized cotton) or similar yarn:

    1 skein in green (main color), approx. 75 yards (75m)
    1 skein in yellow, approx. 10 yards (10m)
    1 black strand

- Two 6mm safety eyes (or black embroidery cotton yarn)
- Stuffing
- Tapestry needle
- Scissors

TECHNIQUES USED

- ch (chain)
- sc (single crochet)
- sl st (slip stitch)
- picot
- inc. (increase)
- dec. (invisible decrease)
- magic ring (page 8)

NOTES

1 This amigurumi is crocheted in the round, unless specified otherwise.

2 If this stuffed animal is for a child, go down one hook size if you crochet loosely.

3 If this stuffed animal is for an infant, replace the safety eyes with embroidered eyes.

INSTRUCTIONS

HEAD AND BODY

In green

Rnd 1: Start with a magic ring
Rnd 2: 6 sc in MR (6 st)
Rnd 3: Inc. in all 6 stitches (12 st)
Rnd 4: *1 sc, Inc.* x 6 (18 st)
Rnd 5: 1 sc, Inc., *2 sc, Inc.* x 5, 1 sc (24 st)
Rnd 6: *3 sc, Inc.* x 6 (30 st)
Rnd 7: SC in each stitch around (30 st)
Rnd 8: 2 sc, Inc., *4 sc, Inc.* x 5, 2 sc (36 st)
Rnd 9: SC in each stitch around (36 st)
Rnd 10: *5 sc, Inc.* x 6 (42 st)
Rnds 11–23: SC in each stitch around (42 st)
Rnd 24: *5 sc, dec.* x 6 (36 st)
Rnd 25: SC in each stitch around (36 st)
Start stuffing.

Rnd 26: 2 sc, dec., *4 sc, dec.* x 5, 2 sc (30 st)
Rnd 27: *3 sc, dec.* x 6 (24 st)
Rnd 28: 1 sc, dec., *2 sc, dec.* x 5, 1 sc (18 st)
Rnd 29: *1 sc, dec.* x 6 (12 st)
Rnd 30: Dec. 6 times (6 st)
Stuff tightly. Cut the yarn and weave it through the remaining 6 stitches using a tapestry needle, pull tight and weave it in. Embroider the mouth on row 8.

EYES

In green

Rnd 1: Start with a magic ring
Rnd 2: 6 sc in MR (6 st)
Rnd 3: Inc. in all 6 stitches (12 st)
Rnds 4–5: SC in each stitch around (12 st)
Insert the safety eyes between rows 4 and 5.
Finish with 1 sl st, then cut the yarn leaving enough length for sewing. Stuff lightly.
Make the second eye the same way.

ARMS

In green

Start by making three fingers, which will be on the end of the arms.

Rnd 1: Start with a magic ring
Rnd 2: 4 sc in MR (4 st)
Finish with 1 sl st, cut the yarn and weave it in for all three fingers.
Rnd 3: Place the three fingers side by side. You'll now crochet around the three fingers to connect them. To do so, crochet 2 stitches from each finger, then continue the round to connect the other 6 stitches on the other side of the fingers, as shown in the diagram below.

Rnd 4: SC in each stitch around (12 st)
Rnd 5: *2 sc, dec.* x 3 (9 st)
Rnd 6: *1 sc, dec.* x 3 (6 st)
Rnd 7: *1 sc, Inc.* x 3 (9 st)
Start stuffing.
Rnds 8–13: SC in each stitch around (9 st)
Rnd 14: *1 sc, dec.* x 3 (6 st)
Stuff lightly. Cut the yarn leaving enough length for sewing and weave it through the remaining 6 stitches using a tapestry needle, pull tight.
Make the second arm the same way.

The eyes

The eyes & the arms

The legs

The crown

THE LEGS

In green

Start by making three toes, which will be on the end of the legs.

Rnd 1: Start with a magic ring

Rnd 2: 4 sc in MR (4 st)

Rnd 3: SC in each stitch around (4 st)

Finish with 1 sl st, cut the yarn and weave it in for all four toes.

Rnd 4: Place the four toes side by side. You'll now crochet around the four toes to connect them. To do so, crochet 2 stitches from each toe, then continue the round to connect the other 8 stitches on the other side of the toes, as shown in the diagram below.

Rnd 5: SC in each stitch around (16 st)

Rnd 6: 2 sc, 2 dec., 4 sc, 2 dec., 2 sc (12 st)

Rnd 7: 6 dec. (6 st)

Rnd 8: 3 sc, [FL] 3 sl st (6 st)

Rnd 9: *2 sc, Inc.* x 2 (8 st)

Start stuffing.

Rnds 10–29: SC in each stitch around (8 st)

Lightly stuff half the leg. Finish with 1 sl st, then cut the yarn leaving enough length for sewing.

Make the second leg the same way.

FINISHING

Sew the eyes to the head between rows 5 and 8.

Sew the arms to the body between rows 11 and 14.

Sew the legs to the body. Sew the non-stuffed part along the body starting at row 27. Around row 18, bend the leg, and sew one stitch to hold it in this position. Repeat on the other leg.

CROWN

In yellow

Row 1: 20 ch

Starting now you'll be working in the round (be careful not to twist the chain): the first stitch of row 2 will be the first stitch of the chain (row 1)

Rnds 2–4: 20 sc (20 st)

Rnd 5: *picot, skip 1 st, 1 sl st* x 10 (20 st)

MR. MINI HEDEGEHOG AND HAIRBRUSH

LEVEL: INTERMEDIATE

SIZE: 4¼″ (11cm)

MATERIALS

- Hook size D/3 (3mm) or whatever matches your yarn, if using a different kind
- Scheepjes Catona Cotton yarn (100% mercerized cotton) or similar yarn:

    1 skein in cream (main color), approx. 60 yards (60m)

    1 skein in light brown, approx. 30 yards (30m)

    1 skein in golden brown, approx. 30 yards (30m)

    1 skein in dark brown, approx. 30 yards (30m)

- Two 6mm safety eyes (or black embroidery cotton yarn)
- Stuffing
- Tapestry needle / Scissors

TECHNIQUES USED

- ch (chain)
- sc (single crochet)
- sl st (slip stitch)
- hdc (half double crochet)
- dc (double crochet)
- inc. (increase)
- dcinc (double crochet increase)
- dec. (invisible decrease)
- FL / BL (front loop / back loop)
- magic ring (page 8)

NOTES

1 This amigurumi is crocheted in the round, unless specified otherwise.

2 If this stuffed animal is for a child, go down one hook size if you crochet loosely.

3 If this stuffed animal is for an infant, replace the safety eyes with embroidered eyes.

INSTRUCTIONS

HEAD AND BODY

In cream

Rnd 1: Start with a magic ring

Rnd 2: 6 sc in MR (6 st)

Rnd 3: Inc. in all 6 stitches (12 st)

Rnd 4: *1 sc, Inc.* x 6 (18 st)

Rnd 5: 1 sc, Inc., *2 sc, Inc.* x 5, 1 sc (24 st)

Rnd 6: *3 sc, Inc.* x 6 (30 st)

Rnd 7: SC in each stitch around (30 st)

Rnd 8: 2 sc, Inc., *4 sc, Inc.* x 5, 2 sc (36 st)

Rnd 9: SC in each stitch around (36 st)

Rnd 10: *5 sc, Inc.* x 6 (42 st)

Rnds 11–26: SC in each stitch around (42 st)

Insert the safety eyes between rows 11 and 12 with 7 stitches in between.

Rnd 27: *5 sc, dec.* x 6 (36 st)

Rnd 28: SC in each stitch around (36 st)

Rnd 29: 2 sc, dec., *4 sc, dec.* x 5, 2 sc (30 st)

The eyes and the snout

The arms and legs

Start stuffing.
Rnd 30: *3 sc, dec.* x 6 (24 st)
Rnd 31: 1 sc, dec., *2 sc, dec.* x 5, 1 sc (18 st)
Rnd 32: *1 sc, dec.* x 6 (12 st)
Rnd 33: Dec. 6 times (6 st)
Stuff tightly. Cut the yarn and weave it through the remaining 6 stitches using a tapestry needle, pull tight and weave it in.

EARS
In cream
Rnd 1: Start with a magic ring
Rnd 2: 6 sc in MR (6 st)
Finish with 1 sl st, then cut the yarn leaving enough length for sewing. Make the second ear the same way.

SNOUT
In cream
Rnd 1: Start with a magic ring
Rnd 2: 3 sc in MR (3 st)
Rnd 3: Inc. in all 3 stitches (6 st)
Rnd 4: *1 sc, Inc.* x 3 (9 st)
Rnd 5: SC in each stitch around (9 st)
Finish with 1 sl st, then cut the yarn leaving enough length for sewing. Embroider the snout with some brown yarn.

ARMS
In cream
Rnd 1: Start with a magic ring
Rnd 2: 6 sc in MR (6 st)
Rnd 3: *1 sc, Inc.* x 3 (9 st)
Rnds 4–7: SC in each stitch around (9 st)
Stuff lightly. Finish with 1 sl st, cut the yarn leaving enough length for sewing.
Make the second arm the same way.

LEGS
In cream
Rnd 1: Start with a magic ring
Rnd 2: 6 sc in MR (6 st)
Rnd 3: Inc. in all 6 stitches (12 st)
Rnd 4: [BL.] SC in each stitch around (12 st)
Rnd 5: SC in each stitch around (12 st)
Rnd 6: 3 sc, 3 dec., 3 sc (9 st)
Rnds 7–9: SC in each stitch around (9 st)
Rnd 10: *1 sc, dec.* x 3 (6 st)
Stuff tightly. Cut the yarn, leaving enough length for sewing, and weave it through the remaining 6 stitches using a tapestry needle. Pull tight. Repeat to make the second leg.

FINISHING

To make the quills, attach 2½″ (6cm) strands of yarn to the body. Start 5 stitches to the side of the eyes and trace a vertical line. Then draw an arc that goes behind the ears and to the top of the head, 6 stitches above the first vertical line. Once this is done you can fill the whole back with strands, all the way to the bottom of the body (page 15).

Sew the snout to the head between rows 12 and 16.

Sew the ears to the head between rows 9 and 11, in front of the quills.

Sew the arms to the body between rows 16 and 20. Sew row 6 of the arm at the junction with the first quill line. Sew the legs to the body around row 33.

HAIRBRUSH
HANDLE

Worked flat in dark brown.

Row 1: 5 ch, turn.

Rows 2–6: 4 sc, 1 ch, turn (4 st)

Row 7: 2 dec., 1 ch, turn (2 st)

Rows 8–12: 2 sc, 1 ch, turn (2 st)

Row 13: SC in each stitch (2 st)

Cut the yarn and weave it in.

Make a second piece the same way, and secure them together with a single crochet row (page 12). This will be the handle and back of the brush.

BRISTLES

In cream

Rnd 1: Start with a magic ring

Rnd 2: 6 sc in MR (6 st)

Rnd 3: {1 hdc, 1 sc}, {1 sc, 1 hdc}, {dcinc}, {1 hdc, 1 sc}, {1 sc, 1 hdc}, {dcinc} (12 st)

Rnd 4: [BL] SC in each stitch around (12 st)

Rnd 5: SC in each stitch around (12 st)

Finish with 1 sl st. Stuff lightly and sew the bristles to the back of the brush centered and around rows 1 to 6.

The quills

The brush

MS. DONKEY AND HAT

LEVEL: INTERMEDIATE

SIZE: 8˝ (20cm)

MATERIALS

- Hook size D/3 (3mm) or whatever matches your yarn, if using a different kind

- Scheepjes Catona Cotton yarn (100% mercerized cotton) or similar yarn:

   1 skein in dark gray, approx. 110 yards (110m)

   1 skein in black, approx. 30 yards (30m)

   1 skein in white, approx. 20 yards (20m)

- Two 6mm safety eyes (or black embroidery cotton yarn)

- Stuffing

- Tapestry needle

- Scissors

POINTS EMPLOYÉS

- ch (chain)
- sc (single crochet)
- sl st (slip stitch)
- inc. (increase)
- dec. (invisible decrease)
- FL / BL (front loop / back loop)
- magic ring (page 8)

NOTES

1 This amigurumi is crocheted in the round, unless specified otherwise.

2 If this stuffed animal is for a child, go down one hook size if you crochet loosely.

3 If this stuffed animal is for an infant, replace the safety eyes with embroidered eyes.

4 There are two options for placing the arms: You may sew them at the end, or, for a more secure finish, you may crochet them at the same time as round 30 of the body (page 14).

INSTRUCTIONS

HEAD

In white and dark gray

Rnd 1: (white) Start with a magic ring

Rnd 2: 6 sc in MR (6 st)

Rnd 3: Inc. in all 6 stitches (12 st)

Rnd 4: *1 sc, Inc. * x 6 (18 st)

Rnd 5: 1 sc, Inc., *2 sc, Inc. * x 5, 1 sc (24 st)

Rnds 6–7: SC in each stitch around (24 st)

Rnd 8: *3 sc, Inc. * x 6 (30 st)

Rnds 9–10: SC in each stitch around (30 st)

Rnd 11: (gray) 2 sc, Inc., *4 sc, Inc. * x 5, 2 sc (36 st)

Rnds 12–13: SC in each stitch around (36 st)

Rnd 14: *5 sc, Inc.* x 6 (42 st)

Rnds 15–16: SC in each stitch around (42 st)

Insert the eyes between rows 16 and 17, with 15 st in between.

Rnd 17: 3 sc, Inc., *6 sc, Inc. * x 5, 3 sc (48 st)

Rnds 18–19: SC in each stitch around (48 st)

Rnd 20: *7 sc, Inc. * x 6 (54 st)
Rnds 21–22: SC in each stitch around (54 st)
Start stuffing.
Rnd 23: *7 sc, dec. * x 6 (48 st)
Rnd 24: 3 sc, dec., *6 sc, dec. * x 5, 3 sc (42 st)
Rnd 25: *5 sc, dec. * x 6 (36 st)
Rnd 26: 2 sc, dec., *4 sc, dec. * x 5, 2 sc (30 st)
Rnd 27: *3 sc, dec. * x 6 (24 st)
Rnd 28: 1 sc, dec., *2 sc, dec. * x 5, 1 sc (18 st)
Rnd 29: *1 sc, dec. * x 6 (12 st)
Rnd 30: Dec. 6 times (6 st)
Stuff tightly. Cut the yarn and weave it through the remaining 6 stitches using a tapestry needle, pull tight and weave it in. Embroider the nostrils with dark gray yarn. Add a few black hairs to the top and back of the head to make a mane (page 15).

EARS
In dark gray
Rnd 1: Start with a magic ring
Rnd 2: 6 sc in MR (6 st)
Rnd 3: *1 sc, Inc.* x 3 (9 st)
Rnd 4: SC in each stitch around (9 st)
Rnd 5: 1 sc, Inc., *2 sc, Inc.* x 2, 1 sc (12 st)
Rnd 6: SC in each stitch around (12 st)
Rnd 7: *1 sc, Inc.* x 6 (18 st)
Rnds 8–14: SC in each stitch around (18 st)
Rnd 15: *7 sc, dec.* x 2 (16 st)
Rnd 16: SC in each stitch around (16 st)
Rnd 17: *6 sc, dec.* x 2 (14 st)
Rnd 18: SC in each stitch around (14 st)
Finish with 1 sl st, then cut the yarn leaving enough length for sewing. Repeat to make the second ear.

ARMS AND HOOFS
In black and dark gray
Rnd 1: (black) Start with a magic ring
Rnd 2: 6 sc in MR (6 st)
Rnd 3: Inc. in all 6 stitches (12 st)
Rnd 4: [BL] SC in each stitch around (12 st)
Rnd 5: 4 sc, 2 dec., 4 sc (10 st)
Rnd 6: (dark gray) SC in each stitch around (10 st)
Rnd 7: 4 sc, dec., 4 sc (9 st)
Rnds 8–11: SC in each stitch around (9 st)
Lightly stuff the hoof. Finish with 1 sl st, then cut the yarn leaving enough length for sewing if you wish to do so, otherwise weave it in.
Repeat to make the second arm and hoof.

BODY
In dark gray
Rnd 1: Start with a magic ring
Rnd 2: 6 sc in MR (6 st)
Rnd 3: Inc. in all 6 stitches (12 st)
Rnd 4: *1 sc, Inc.* x 6 (18 st)
Rnd 5: 1 sc, Inc., *2 sc, Inc.* x 5, 1 sc (24 st)
Rnd 6: *3 sc, Inc.* x 6 (30 st)
Rnd 7: 2 sc, Inc., *4 sc, Inc.* x 5, 2 sc (36 st)
Rnd 8: *5 sc, Inc.* x 6 (42 st)
Rnd 9: 3 sc, Inc., *6 sc, Inc.* x 5, 3 sc (48 st)
Rnd 10: *7 sc, Inc.* x 6 (54 st)
Rnd 11: 4 sc, Inc., *8 sc, Inc.* x 5, 4 sc (60 st)
Rnds 12–16: SC in each stitch around (60 st)
Rnd 17: 4 sc, dec., *8 sc, dec.* x 5, 4 sc (54 st)

Rnds 18–19: SC in each stitch around (54 st)
Rnd 20: *7 sc, dec.* x 6 (48 st)
Rnds 21–22: SC in each stitch around (48 st)
Rnd 23: 3 sc, dec., *6 sc, dec.* x 5, 3 sc (42 st)
Start stuffing.
Rnds 24–25: SC in each stitch around (42 st)
Rnd 26: *5 sc, dec.* x 6 (36 st)
Rnds 27–29: SC in each stitch around (36 st)
Rnd 30: 2 sc, dec., *4 sc, dec.* x 5, 2 sc (30 st)
Attach the arms (page 14).
Rnds 31–33: SC in each stitch around (30 st)
Stuff tightly. Finish with 1 sl st then cut the yarn leaving enough length for sewing.

LEGS
In black and dark gray
Rnd 1: (black) Start with a magic ring
Rnd 2: 6 sc in MR (6 st)
Rnd 3: Inc. in all 6 stitches (12 st)
Rnd 4: *1 sc, Inc.* x 6 (18 st)
Rnd 5: [BL] SC in each stitch around (18 st)
Rnd 6: 6 sc, 3 dec., 6 sc (15 st)
Start stuffing.
Rnd 7: (dark gray) SC in each stitch around (15 st)
Rnd 8: 5 sc, 3 dec., 4 sc (12 st)
Rnds 9–11: SC in each stitch around (12 st)
Rnd 12: Dec 6 times (6 st)
Stuff lightly. Finish with 1 sl st and cut the yarn leaving enough length for sewing.
Repeat to make the second leg.

The legs

The Tail

The hat

TAIL

In black and dark gray

Rnd 1: (black) Start with a magic ring

Rnd 2: 6 sc in MR (6 st)

Rnd 3: Inc. in all 6 stitches (12 st)

Rnds 4–6: SC in each stitch around (12 st)

Rnd 7: *4 sc, dec.* x 2 (10 st)

Rnd 8: SC in each stitch around (10 st)

Rnd 9: *3 sc, dec.* x 2 (8 st)

Rnds 10–17: (dark gray) SC in each stitch around (8 st)

Lightly stuff the black tip. Finish with 1 sl st then cut the yarn leaving enough length for sewing. Add black strands of yarn to cover the black tip of the tail (page 15).

FINISHING

You should have left enough yarn when finishing the body to sew it to the head. Simply place the head on the opening of the body and finish stuffing tightly, then sew them together.

Sew the ears to the head between rows 21 and 23, folding them in half to make them hollow at the base.

Sew the arms to the body around row 30 if you haven't already attached them while making the body.

Sew the legs to the base of the body around row 4. Make sure the amigurumi is stable.

Sew the tail to the back of the body between rows 7 and 10.

HAT

In white

Row 1: 24 ch. You'll now be working in the round (be careful not to twist the chain). The first stitch of Rnd 2 will be the first stitch of the chain (row 1)

Rnds 2–6: SC in each stitch around (24 st)

Rnd 7: 6 sc, do not work the next 12 st, 6 sc (12 st)

Rnds 8–10: SC in each stitch around (12 st)

Rnd 11: *4 sc, dec.* x 2 (10 st)

Rnd 12: SC in each stitch around (10 st)

Rnd 13: *3 sc, dec.* x 2 (8 st)

Rnd 14: SC in each stitch around (8 st)

Rnd 15: *2 sc, dec.* x 2 (6 st)

Cut the yarn and weave it through the remaining 6 stitches using a tapestry needle, pull tight and weave it in. Now, work the 12 stitches set aside during Rnd 7: do one round of sc, then repeat rows 8 to 15. Cut the yarn and weave it through the remaining 6 stitches using a tapestry needle, pull tight and weave it in.

MR. WOLF
AND BROCCOLI

LEVEL: INTERMEDIATE

SIZE: 8″ (20cm)

MATERIALS

- Hook size D/3 (3mm) or whatever matches your yarn, if using a different kind
- Scheepjes Catona Cotton yarn (100% mercerized cotton) or similar yarn:

    1 skein in light gray, approx.
      120 yards (120m)
    1 skein in white, approx. 25 yards (25m)
    1 skein in black, approx. 2 yards (2m)
    1 skein in light green, approx. 5 yards (5m)
    1 skein in dark green, approx. 15 yards (15m)

- Two 6mm safety eyes (or black embroidery cotton yarn)
- Stuffing
- Tapestry needle
- Scissors

TECHNIQUES USED

- ch (chain)
- sc (single crochet)
- sl st (slip stitch)
- dc (double crochet)
- inc. (increase)
- dec. (invisible decrease)
- FL / BL (front loop / back loop)
- magic ring (page 8)

NOTES

1 This amigurumi is crocheted in the round, unless specified otherwise.

2 If this stuffed animal is for a child, go down one hook size if you crochet loosely.

3 If this stuffed animal is for an infant, replace the safety eyes with embroidered eyes.

4 There are two options for placing the arms: You may sew them at the end, or, for a more secure finish, you may crochet them at the same time as round 30 of the body (page 14).

INSTRUCTIONS

HEAD

In light gray and white

Rnd 1: (white) Start with a magic ring
Rnd 2: 6 sc in MR (6 st)
Rnd 3: Inc. in all 6 stitches (12 st)
Rnd 4: *1 sc, Inc.* x 6 (18 st)
Rnd 5: *5 sc, Inc.* x 3 (21 st)
Rnd 6: SC in each stitch around (21 st)
Rnd 7: *6 sc, Inc.* x 3 (24 st)
Rnd 8: SC in each stitch around (24 st)
Rnd 9: *7 sc, Inc.* x 3 (27 st)
Rnd 10: SC in each stitch around (27 st)
Rnd 11: *8 sc, Inc.* x 3 (30 st)
Rnd 12: SC in each stitch around (30 st)
Rnd 13: (gray) 2 sc, Inc., *4 sc, Inc.* x 5, 2 sc (36 st)
Insert the eyes between rows 13 and 14 (with 9 st in between).

Rnd 14: *5 sc, Inc.* x 6 (42 st)
Rnd 15: SC in each stitch around (42 st)
Rnd 16: 3 sc, Inc., *6 sc, Inc.* x 5, 3 sc (48 st)
Rnd 17: SC in each stitch around (48 st)
Rnd 18: *7 sc, Inc.* x 6 (54 st)
Rnds 19–20: SC in each stitch around (54 st)
Start stuffing.
Rnd 21: *7 sc, dec.* x 6 (48 st)
Rnd 22: 3 sc, dec., *6 sc, dec.* x 5, 3 sc (42 st)
Rnd 23: *5 sc, dec.* x 6 (36 st)
Rnd 24: 2 sc, dec., *4 sc, dec.* x 5, 2 sc (30 st)
Rnd 25: *3 sc, dec.* x 6 (24 st)
Rnd 26: 1 sc, dec., *2 sc, dec.* x 5, 1 sc (18 st)
Rnd 27: *1 sc, dec.* x 6 (12 st)
Rnd 28: Dec. 6 times (6 st)
Stuff tightly. Cut the yarn and weave it through the remaining 6 stitches using a tapestry needle, pull tight and weave it in. Embroider the snout with some black yarn.

EARS

In light gray
Rnd 1: Start with a magic ring
Rnd 2: 3 sc in MR (3 st)
Rnd 3: Inc. in all 3 stitches (6 st)
Rnd 4: SC in each stitch around (6 st)
Rnd 5: *1 sc, Inc.* x 3 (9 st)
Rnd 6: 1 sc, Inc., *2 sc, Inc.* x 2, 1 sc (12 st)
Rnd 7: SC in each stitch around (12 st)
Rnd 8: *3 sc, Inc.* x 3 (15 st)
Rnd 9: 2 sc, Inc., *4 sc, Inc.* x 2, 2 sc (18 st)
Rnd 10: SC in each stitch around (18 st)
Rnd 11: *5 sc, Inc.* x 3 (21 st)
Rnd 12: SC in each stitch around (21 st)

Finish with 1 sl st, then cut the yarn leaving enough length for sewing. Repeat to make the second ear.

ARMS

In white and light gray
Rnd 1: (white) Start with a magic ring
Rnd 2: 6 sc in MR (6 st)
Rnd 3: *1 sc, Inc.* x 3 (9 st)
Rnds 4–6: SC in each stitch around (9 st)
Rnds 7–12: (light gray) SC in each stitch around (9 st)
Finish with 1 sl st, then cut the yarn leaving enough length for sewing if you wish to do so, otherwise weave it in. No need to stuff.
Repeat to make the second arm.

BODY

In light gray
Rnd 1: Start with a magic ring
Rnd 2: 6 sc in MR (6 st)
Rnd 3: Inc. in all 6 stitches (12 st)
Rnd 4: *1 sc, Inc.* x 6 (18 st)
Rnd 5: 1 sc, Inc., *2 sc, Inc.* x 5, 1 sc (24 st)
Rnd 6: *3 sc, Inc.* x 6 (30 st)
Rnd 7: 2 sc, Inc., *4 sc, Inc.* x 5, 2 sc (36 st)
Rnd 8: *5 sc, Inc.* x 6 (42 st)
Rnd 9: 3 sc, Inc., *6 sc, Inc.* x 5, 3 sc (48 st)
Rnd 10: *7 sc, Inc.* x 6 (54 st)
Rnd 11: 4 sc, Inc., *8 sc, Inc.* x 5, 4 sc (60 st)
Rnds 12–16: SC in each stitch around (60 st)
Rnd 17: 4 sc, dec., *8 sc, dec.* x 5, 4 sc (54 st)

Rnds 18–19: SC in each stitch around (54 st)
Rnd 20: *7 sc, dec.* x 6 (48 st)
Rnds 21–22: SC in each stitch around (48 st)
Start stuffing.
Rnd 23: 3 sc, dec., *6 sc, dec.* x 5, 3 sc (42 st)
Rnds 24–25: SC in each stitch around (42 st)
Rnd 26: *5 sc, dec.* x 6 (36 st)
Rnds 27–29: SC in each stitch around (36 st)
Rnd 30: 2 sc, dec., *4 sc, dec.* x 5, 2 sc (30 st)
Attach the arms (page 14).
Rnds 31–33: SC in each stitch around (30 st)
Stuff tightly. Finish with 1 sl st then cut the yarn leaving enough length for sewing.

LEGS

In white and light gray
Rnd 1: (white) Start with a magic ring
Rnd 2: 6 sc in MR (6 st)
Rnd 3: Inc. in all 6 stitches (12 st)
Rnd 4: *1 sc, Inc.* x 6 (18 st)
Rnd 5: [BL] SC in each stitch around (18 st)
Rnd 6: 6 sc, 3 dec., 6 sc (15 st)
Start stuffing.
Rnd 7: (light gray) SC in each stitch around (15 st)
Rnd 8: 5 sc, 3 dec., 4 sc (12 st)
Rnds 9–11: SC in each stitch around (12 st)
Rnd 12: Dec. 6 times (6 st)
Stuff tightly. Cut the yarn, leaving enough length for sewing, and weave it through the remaining 6 stitches using

a tapestry needle. Pull tight.
Repeat to make the second leg.

TAIL

In white and light gray

Rnd 1: (white) Start with a magic ring
Rnd 2: 3 sc in MR (3 st)
Rnd 3: Inc. in all 3 stitches (6 st)
Rnd 4: *1 sc, Inc.* x 3 (9 st)
Rnd 5: 1 sc, Inc., *2 sc, Inc.* x 2, 1 sc (12 st)
Rnd 6: *3 sc, Inc.* x 3 (15 st)
Rnd 7: 2 sc, Inc., *4 sc, Inc.* x 2, 2 sc (18 st)
Rnds 8–10: SC in each stitch around (18 st)
Rnds 11–16: (light gray) SC in each stitch around (18 st)
Rnd 17: *7 sc, dec.* x 2 (16 st)
Start stuffing.
Rnd 18: SC in each stitch around (16 st)
Rnd 19: *6 sc, dec.* x 2 (14 st)
Rnd 20: SC in each stitch around (14 st)
Rnd 21: *5 sc, dec.* x 2 (12 st)
Rnd 22: SC in each stitch around (12 st)
Rnd 23: Dec. 6 times (6 st)
Stuff tightly. Cut the yarn leaving enough length for sewing and weave it through the remaining 6 stitches using a tapestry needle.

FINISHING

You should have left enough yarn when finishing the body to sew it to the head. Simply place the head on the opening of the body and finish stuffing tightly, then sew them together.

Sew the ears to the head between rows 19 and 22. Fold them in half slightly to make them hollow at the base.
Sew the arms to the body around row 30 if you haven't already attached them while making the body.
Sew the legs to the body around row 3.
Sew the tail to the back of the body above row 1.

BROCCOLI

THE STEM

In light green

Rnd 1: Start with a magic ring
Rnd 2: 6 sc in MR (6 st)
Rnd 3: Inc. in all 6 stitches (12 st)
Rnd 4: [BL] SC in each stitch around (12 st)
Rnds 5–9: SC in each stitch around (12 st)
Rnd 10: [BL] Dec. 6 times (6 st)
Stuff tightly.
Cut the yarn and weave it through the remaining 6 stitches using a tapestry

needle, making sure to go through the back of the loop. Pull tight and weave the yarn in.

THE BROCCOLI CROWN

In dark green

Since you worked the last two rounds in the back loop of the stem (Rnd 10 and the closing round), the front loops should be visible. Next:
Switch to dark green yarn and insert your hook into the first front loop of the closing round and crochet as follows: {4 ch, *1 dc, 1 ch * x 5}
In the next 5 loops (which make up the first circle), crochet as follows: {*1 dc, 1 ch * x 6}
In the next 12 loops (which make up the larger circle from round 10), crochet as follows: {*1 dc, 1 ch * x 8}
Finish with 1 sl st, cut the yarn and weave it in.

The Tail

The broccoli

MS. PENGUIN AND FLOATIE

LEVEL: **EXPERT**

SIZE: **8˝ (20cm)**

MATERIALS

- Hook size D/3 (3mm) or whatever matches your yarn, if using a different kind
- Scheepjes Catona Cotton yarn (100% mercerized cotton) or similar yarn:

  1 skein in black (main color), approx. 100 yards (100m)

  1 skein in white (main color), approx. 40 yards (40m)

  1 skein in yellow, approx. 60 yards (60m)

  1 orange strand

- Two 6mm safety eyes (or black embroidery cotton yarn)
- Stuffing
- Tapestry needle
- Scissors

TECHNIQUES USED

- ch (chain)
- sc (single crochet)
- csc (center single crochet) (page 13)
- sl st (slip stitch)
- inc. (increase)
- dec. (invisible decrease)
- FL / BL (front loop / back loop)
- magic ring (page 8)

NOTES

1 This amigurumi is crocheted in the round, unless specified otherwise.

2 If this stuffed animal is for a child, go down one hook size if you crochet loosely.

3 If this stuffed animal is for an infant, replace the safety eyes with embroidered eyes.

INSTRUCTIONS

BODY AND HEAD

In black, white and yellow

IMPORTANT: The following instructions are for EACH round.

Each round will be half black, half white. For instance, for round 1, you'll do 3 sc in black, then 3 sc in white. For round 2 you'll do 3 Inc. in black, then 3 Inc. in white. For round 3, you'll do *1 sc, Inc.* x 3 in black, then *1 sc, Inc.* x 3 in white.

I recommend carrying the second yarn for more ease (carrying means twisting the secondary yarn with the working yarn so it follows as you crochet). Since black yarn shows more through the white, it's better to carry it only two or three times throughout the round. This technique is not mandatory, but if you choose not to do it, then remember to keep enough slack when you switch to the second yarn. Also, remember to untangle the yarn at the end of each row so it doesn't turn into knots.

When you've reached the last stitch before a color change, in the middle and at the end of each row, work a center single crochet stitch (or center increase) for a neat color change. Don't forget to switch yarn during the last step of your stitch-making (page 13).

The head

The beak

Rnd 1: (black) Start with a magic ring

Rnd 2: (black and white) 6 sc in MR (6 st)

Rnd 3: Inc. in all 6 stitches (12 st)

Rnd 4: *1 sc, Inc.* x 6 (18 st)

Rnd 5: 1 sc, Inc., *2 sc, Inc.* x 5, 1 sc (24 st)

Rnd 6: *3 sc, Inc.* x 6 (30 st)

Rnd 7: 2 sc, Inc., *4 sc, Inc.* x 5, 2 sc (36 st)

Rnd 8: *5 sc, Inc.* x 6 (42 st)

Rnd 9: 3 sc, Inc., *6 sc, Inc.* x 5, 3 sc (48 st)

Rnd 20: *7 sc, Inc.* x 6 (54 st)

Rnd 12: 4 sc, Inc., *8 sc, Inc.* x 5, 4 sc (60 st)

Rnds 12–16: SC in each stitch around (60 st)

Rnd 17: 4 sc, dec., *8 sc, dec.* x 5, 4 sc (54 st)

Rnds 18–19: SC in each stitch around (54 st)

Rnd 20: *dec., 7 sc * x 6 (48 st)

Rnds 21–22: SC in each stitch around (48 st)

Rnd 23: 3 sc, dec., *6 sc, dec.* x 5, 3 sc (42 st)

Start stuffing.

Rnds 24–25: SC in each stitch around (42 st)

Rnd 26: *dec., 5 sc* x 6 (36 st)

Rnds 27–29: SC in each stitch around (36 st)

Rnd 30: 2 sc, dec., *4 sc, dec.* x 5, 2 sc (30 st)

Rnd 31: SC in each stitch around (30 st)

Rnds 32–34: (black and yellow) SC in each stitch around (30 st)

Rnd 35: (black) 2 sc, Inc, *4 sc, Inc.* x 5, 2 sc (36 st)

Keep doing the center single crochet stitches on this last round even though it's a single color.

Starting now, you'll be working only with black. No more center single crochet.

Rnd 36: (black) *5 sc, Inc.* x 6 (42 st)

Rnds 37–44: SC in each stitch around (42 st)

Insert the eyes between rows 42 and 43 (with 12 stitches in between).

Rnd 45: *5 sc, dec.* x 6 (36 st)

Rnd 46: 2 sc, dec., *4 sc, dec.* x 5, 2 sc (30 st)

Rnd 47: *3 sc, dec.* x 6 (24 st)

Rnd 48: 1 sc, dec., *2 sc, dec.* x 5, 1 sc (18 st)

Keep stuffing.

Rnd 49: *1 sc, dec.* x 6 (12 st)

Rnd 50: Dec 6 times (6 st)

Stuff tightly. Cut the yarn and weave it through the remaining 6 stitches using a tapestry needle, pull tight and weave it in.

BEAK

In yellow

Rnd 1: Start with a magic ring

Rnd 2: 6 sc in MR (6 st)

Rnd 3: SC in each stitch around (6 st)

Rnd 4: *1 sc, Inc.* x 3 (9 st)

Rnd 5: SC in each stitch around (9 st)

Rnd 6: 1 sc, Inc., *2 sc, Inc.* x 2, 1 sc (12 st)

Rnds 7–10: SC in each stitch around (12 st)

Stuff tightly. Finish with 1 sl st. Cut the yarn, leaving enough length for sewing.

WINGS

Worked flat. Make 2 black and 2 white wings.

Row 1: 3 ch, turn

Rows 2–5: 2 sc, 1 ch, turn (2 st)

Row 6: 1 sc, Inc., 1 ch, turn (3 st)

Row 7: Inc., 2 sc, 1 ch, turn (4 st)

Row 8: 2 sc, dec., 1 ch, turn (3 st)

Row 9: dec., 1 sc, 1 ch, turn (2 st)

Rows 10–14: 2 sc, 1 ch, turn (2 st)

Row 15: SC in each stitch around (2 st)

Cut the yarn and weave it in.

Once you have all four made, take one white wing and one black wing, place them on top of each other and secure them together by crocheting a sc row all around the wing (page 12). *REMEMBER to flip the second wings, so they face the other way.*

Cut all strands of yarn and weave them in.

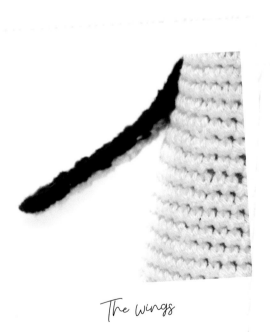

The wings

The wings seen from the back

FEET

In yellow

Start by making three toes, which will shape the end of the feet.

Rnd 1: Start with a magic ring

Rnd 2: 4 sc in MR (4 st)

Finish with 1 sl st, cut the yarn and weave it in for all three toes.

Rnd 3: Place the three toes side by side. You'll now crochet around the three toes to connect them. To do so, crochet 2 stitches from each toe, then continue the round to connect the other 6 stitches on the other side of the toes, as shown in the diagram below.

Rnd 4: SC in each stitch around (12 st)

Rnds 5–7: SC in each stitch around (12 st)

Rnd 8: *2 sc, dec.* x 3 (9 st)

Rnd 9: SC in each stitch around (9 st)

Rnd 10: *1 sc, dec.* x 3 (6 st)

Stuff lightly. Cut the yarn and weave it through the remaining 6 stitches, pull tight.

Make the second foot the same way.

TAIL

In black

Rnd 1: Start with a magic ring

Rnd 2: 6 sc in MR (6 st)

Rnd 3: Inc. in all 6 stitches (12 st)

Rnd 4: SC in each stitch around (12 st)

Rnd 5: *1 sc, Inc.* x 6 (18 st)

Rnd 6: SC in each stitch around (18 st)

Rnd 7: 8 sc, 2 Inc., 8 sc (20 st)

Rnd 8: 9 sc, 2 Inc., 9 sc (22 st)

Stuff tightly. Finish with 1 sl st. Cut the yarn leaving enough length for sewing.

The feet

The tail

The floatie

Ms. Penguin

FINISHING

Sew the beak to the head between rows 38 and 42.
Sew the wings to the body under row 30.
Sew the feet to the body around row 5.
Sew the tail to the body between row 7 and 13.

FLOATIE

In yellow, orange and black

THE RING

Row 1: (yellow) Start with a 12 st chain. You'll now be working in the round. The first stitch of Rnd 2 is the first stitch of the chain. Be careful not to twist the chain.

Rnd 2: SC in each stitch around (12 st) Repeat round 2 until the piece measures 13″ (33cm) (make sure it's long enough to wrap around the penguin). Stuff and sew the stitches of the last row and those of the first row together to finish the floatie.

THE DUCK HEAD

Rnd 1: (yellow) Start with a magic ring

Rnd 2: 6 sc in MR (6 st)

Rnd 3: Inc. in all 6 stitches (12 st)

Rnd 4: *1 sc, Inc.* x 6 (18 st)

Rnd 5: 1 sc, Inc., *2 sc, Inc.* x 5, 1 sc (24 st)

Rnds 6–8: SC in each stitch around (24 st)

Rnd 9: 1 sc, dec., *2 sc, dec.* x 5, 1 sc (18 st)

Rnd 10: *1 sc, dec.* x 6 (12 st)

Rnd 11: Dec. 6 times (6 st)

Finish with 1 sl st. Cut the yarn, leaving enough length for sewing. Embroider the eyes with black yarn. For the beak, make a 6-st magic ring with orange yarn and close it with 1 sl st. Stuff and sew the head to the floatie.

MR. MINI SHEEP AND FOX BLANKIE

LEVEL: **EXPERT**

SIZE: 4¾″ (12cm)

MATERIALS

- Hook size D/3 (3mm) or whatever matches your yarn, if using a different kind
- Scheepjes Catona Cotton yarn (100% mercerized cotton) or similar yarn:

    1 skein in cream (main color), approx. 80 yards (80m)
    1 skein in dark brown, approx. 45 yards (45m)
    1 skein in rust, approx. 10 yards (10m)
    1 black strand

- Two 6mm safety eyes (or black embroidery cotton yarn)
- Stuffing
- Tapestry needle
- Scissors

TECHNIQUES USED

- ch (chain)
- sc (single crochet)
- sl st (slip stitch)
- bo (bobble stitch)
- picot
- inc. (increase)
- dec. (invisible decrease)
- FL / BL (front loop / back loop)
- magic ring (page 8)

NOTES

1 This amigurumi is crocheted in the round, unless specified otherwise.

2 If this stuffed animal is for a child, go down one hook size if you crochet loosely.

3 If this stuffed animal is for an infant, replace the safety eyes with embroidered eyes.

INSTRUCTIONS

HEAD AND BODY

In cream and dark brown

Rnd 1: (brown) Start with a magic ring
Rnd 2: 6 sc in MR (6 st)
Rnd 3: Inc. in all 6 stitches (12 st)
Rnd 4: *1 sc, Inc.* x 6 (18 st)
Rnd 5: 1 sc, Inc., *2 sc, Inc.* x 5, 1 sc (24 st)
Rnd 6: *3 sc, Inc.* x 6 (30 st)
Rnd 7: SC in each stitch around (30 st)
Rnd 8: 2 sc, Inc., *4 sc, Inc.* x 5, 2 sc (36 st)
Rnd 9: SC in each stitch around (36 st)
Rnd 10: *5 sc, Inc.* x 6 (42 st)
Rnds 11–15: SC in each stitch around (42 st)
Insert the eyes between rows 11 and 12, with 7 stitches in between. Embroider the nose right under.
Rnd 16: (cream) *1 bo, 1 sc* x 21 (42 st)
Rnd 17: SC in each stitch around (42 st)
Rnd 18: *1 bo, 1 sc* x 21 (42 st)
Rnd 19: SC in each stitch around (42 st)

Rnd 20: *1 bo, 1 sc* x 21 (42 sl)
Rnd 21: SC in each stitch around (42 st)
Rnd 22: *1 bo, 1 sc* x 21 (42 st)
Rnd 23: SC in each stitch around (42 st)
Start stuffing.
Rnd 24: *1 bo, 1 sc* x 21 (42 st)
Rnd 25: SC in each stitch around (42 st)
Rnd 26: *1 bo, 1 sc* x 21 (42 st)
Rnd 27: *5 sc, dec.* x 6 (36 st)
Rnd 28: *1 bo, 1 sc* x 18 (36 st)
Rnd 29: 2 sc, dec., *4 sc, dec.* x 5, 2 sc (30 st)
Rnd 30: *1 bo, 1 sc, 1 bo, dec.* x 6 (24 st)
Rnd 31: 1 sc, dec., *2 sc, dec.* x 5, 1 sc (18 st)

Rnd 32: *1 bo, dec.* x 6 (12 st)
Rnd 33: Dec. 6 times (6 st)
Stuff tightly. Cut the yarn and weave it through the remaining 6 stitches using a tapestry needle, pull tight and weave it in.

BEANIE

In cream
Rnd 1: Start with a magic ring
Rnd 2: 6 sc in MR (6 st)
Rnd 3: {1 bo, 1 sc} x 6 (12 st)
Rnd 4: Inc. in all 12 stitches (24 st)
Rnd 5: *1 bo, 1 sc* x 12 (24 st)

Rnd 6: *1 sc, Inc.* x 12 (36 st)
Rnd 7: *1 bo, 1 sc* x 18 (36 st)
Rnd 8: SC in each stitch around (36 st)
Rnd 9: *1 bo, 1 sc* x 18 (36 st)
Rnd 10: SC in each stitch around (36 st)
Make sure you crochet this last row loosely.
Finish with 1 sl st, then cut the yarn leaving enough length for sewing.

The head

The beanie

The ears

The arms

EARS

In cream and dark brown

Rnd 1: (cream) Start with a magic ring
Rnd 2: 6 sc in MR (6 st)
Rnd 3: Inc. in all 6 stitches (12 st)
Rnd 4: *1 sc, Inc.* x 6 (18 st)
Rnd 5: 1 sc, Inc., *2 sc, Inc.* x 5, 1 sc (24 st)
Make another cream circle, then repeat to make two brown circles. For the cream circles only, cut the yarn and weave it in.
Take one cream circle and one brown circle, place them wrong sides facing each other (with the right side of the brown circle facing you), and secure them together by crocheting a 5th round with brown yarn through both layers simultaneously (page 12):
Rnd 6: *3 sc, Inc.* x 6 (30 st)
Fold the ear in half and crochet 4 stitches together through both layers to keep them folded. Finish with 1 sl st, then cut the yarn leaving enough length for sewing.

ARMS

In brown

Rnd 1: Start with a magic ring
Rnd 2: 6 sc in MR (6 st)
Rnd 3: *1 sc, Inc.* x 3 (9 st)
Rnds 4–9: SC in each stitch around (9 st)
Rnd 10: *1 sc, dec.* x 3 (6 st)
Stuff lightly. Cut the yarn leaving enough length for sewing and weave it through the remaining 6 stitches using a tapestry needle, pull tight. Repeat to make the second arm.

LEGS

In brown

Rnd 1: Start with a magic ring
Rnd 2: 6 sc in MR (6 st)
Rnd 3: Inc. in all 6 stitches (12 st)
Rnd 4: [BL] SC in each stitch around (12 st)
Rnd 5: SC in each stitch around (12 st)
Rnd 6: 3 sc, 3 dec., 3 sc (9 st)
Rnds 7–9: SC in each stitch around (9 st)
Rnd 10: *1 sc, dec.* x 3 (6 st)
Stuff lightly. Cut the yarn leaving enough length for sewing and weave it through the remaining 6 stitches using a tapestry needle, pull tight. Make the second leg the same way.

TAIL

In cream

Rnd 1: Start with a magic ring
Rnd 2: 6 sc in MR (6 st)
Rnd 3: Inc. in all 6 stitches (12 st)
Rnds 4–5: SC in each stitch around (12 st)
Stuff tightly, finish with 1 sl st, then cut the yarn leaving enough length for sewing.

FINISHING

Sew the beanie to the head. Place it slightly back so that you can sew the back edge of the beanie to the first row of bobble stitch (row 16 on the back of the body). In the front, it should be sewn one row above the eyes.
Sew the ears to row 7 of the beanie.
Sew the arms to the body between row 17 and 19.
Sew the legs to the body around row 33.
Sew the tail to the back of the body between row 27 and 30.

The legs

The Tail

Mr. Mini Sheep

The fox blankie

FOX BLANKIE

HEAD

In rust, cream and black

Rnd 1: (rust) Start with a magic ring

Rnd 2: 6 sc in MR (6 st)

Rnd 3: *1 sc, Inc.* (9 st)

Rnd 4: 4 sc, picot, 1 sc, picot, 4 sc (9 st)

Work around the picots so that they stick up. If they move to the wrong side of the work, pop them back through to the front before stuffing.

Rnds 5–6: SC in each stitch around (9 st)

Start stuffing.

Rnd 7: *1 sc, dec.* x 3 (6 st)

Rnd 8: (cream) SC in each stitch around (6 st)

Stuff tightly. Cut the yarn and weave a black strand, together with the beige one, through the remaining 6 stitches using a tapestry needle. Pull tight, tie a knot and weave it in. Embroider two little eyes with black yarn.

BODY

Worked flat in rust

Row 1: 10 ch, turn

Rows 2–10: 9 sc, 1 ch, turn (9 st)

Cut the yarn and weave it in. Sew the head to the middle of one of the sides of the square piece.

MR. SQUID AND BOOK

LEVEL: EXPERT

SIZE: 7½″ (19cm)

MATERIALS

- Hook size D/3 (3mm) or whatever matches your yarn, if using a different kind
- Scheepjes Catona Cotton yarn (100% mercerized cotton) or similar yarn:

    1 skein in blue, approx. 160 yards (160m)
    1 skein in gold, approx. 60 yards (60m)
    1 skein in white, approx. 10 yards (10m)

- Two 6mm safety eyes (or black embroidery cotton yarn)
- Stuffing
- Tapestry needle
- Scissors

TECHNIQUES USED

- ch (chain)
- sc (single crochet)
- sl st (slip stitch)
- dc (double crochet)
- inc. (increase)
- dcinc (double crochet increase)
- dec. (invisible decrease)
- FL / BL (front loop / back loop)
- magic ring (page 8)

NOTES

1 This amigurumi is crocheted in the round, unless specified otherwise.

2 If this stuffed animal is for a child, go down one hook size if you crochet loosely.

3 If this stuffed animal is for an infant, replace the safety eyes with embroidered eyes.

4 There are two options for placing the arms: You may sew them at the end, or, for a more secure finish, you may crochet them at the same time as round 71 of the body (page 14).

INSTRUCTIONS

HEAD

In blue

Rnd 1: Start with a magic ring
Rnd 2: 6 sc in MR (6 st)
Rnd 3: Inc. in all 6 stitches (12 st)
Rnd 4: *1 sc, inc.* x 6 (18 st)
Rnd 5: 1 sc, inc., *2 sc, inc.* x 5, 1 sc (24 st)
Rnd 6: *3 sc, inc.* x 6 (30 st)
Rnd 7: 2 sc, inc., *4 sc, inc.* x 5, 2 sc (36 st)
Rnd 8: *5 sc, inc.* x 6 (42 st)
Rnd 9: 3 sc, inc., *6 sc, inc.* x 5, 3 sc (48 st)
Rnd 10: *7 sc, inc.* x 6 (54 st)
Rnds 11–16: SC in each stitch around (54 st)
The eyes go between row 15 and 16 (with 10 st in between), but wait until you've made the tentacles before adding them.

The head

The arms

Rnd 17: 22 sc, *1 sc, 10 ch. Starting now, you'll be crocheting along your chain: 1 dc in the 3rd chain from the hook, then 4 dc in the next chain, 2 dcinc, 6 dc (the extra dc in the first sc stitch makes it so there is no hole), 1 sc* x 5, 22 sc

Rnd 18: 23 sc, *1 sc, 10 ch. Starting now, you'll be crocheting along your chain: 1 dc in the 3rd stitch from the hook, then 4 dc in the same stitch, 2 dcinc, 6dc (the extra dc in the first sc stitch makes it so there is no hole), 1 sc* x 4, 23 sc

The tentacles are being worked on round 17 and 18 at the same time as the head. At round 18, there are 2 sc stitches between each tentacle from round 17. You will crochet the tentacles of round 18 in those stitches, so they will be off-centered from the tentacles in round 17.

Rnd 19: *7 sc, dec.* x 6 (48 st)
Crochet carefully to make sure you don't drop any stitches.

Rnd 20: 3 sc, dec., *6 sc, dec.* x 5, 3 sc (42 st)

Rnd 21: *5 sc, dec.* x 6 (36 st)
Start stuffing.

Rnd 22: 2 sc, dec., *4 sc, dec.* x 5, 2 sc (30 st)

Rnd 23: *3 sc, dec.* x 6 (24 st)

Rnd 24: 1 sc, dec., *2 sc, dec.* x 5, 1 sc (18 st)

Rnd 25: *1 sc, dec.* x 6 (12 st)

Rnd 26: Dec. 6 times. (6 st)
Stuff tightly. Cut the yarn and weave it through the remaining 6 stitches using a tapestry needle, pull tight and weave it in.

ARMS
In gold and blue
Rnd 1: (gold) Start with a magic ring
Rnd 2: 6 sc in MR (6 st)
Rnd 3: *1 sc, Inc.* x 3 (9 st)
Rnds 4–6: SC in each stitch around (9 st)
Rnds 7–12: (blue) SC in each stitch around (9 st)
Finish with 1 sl st, then cut the yarn leaving enough length for sewing if you wish to do so, otherwise weave it in. No need to stuff.
Repeat to make the second arm.

BODY

In gold and blue

Rnd 1: (gold) Start with a magic ring

Rnd 2: 8 sc in MR (8 st)

Rnd 3: Inc. in all 8 stitches (16 st)

Rnd 4: *1 sc, Inc.* x 8 (24 st)

Rnd 5: 1 sc, Inc., *2 sc, Inc.* x 7, 1 sc (32 st)

Rnd 6: *3 sc, Inc.* x 8 (40 st)

Rnd 7: 2 sc, Inc., *4 sc, Inc.* x 7, 2 sc (48 st)

Rnd 8: *5 sc, Inc.* x 8 (56 st)

Now that you've crocheted the bottom, you're going to crochet the tentacles flat. Make the first one with the same yarn you've been working with. For the other seven tentacles, you'll have to cut the yarn and start with a new piece.

Rows 9–12: 7 sc, 1 ch, turn

Row 13: dec., 5 sc, 1 ch, turn (6 st)

Rows 14–16: 6 sc, 1 ch, turn

Row 17: 4 sc, dec., 1 ch, turn (5 st)

Rows 18–20: 5 sc, 1 ch, turn

Row 21: dec., 3 sc, 1 ch, turn (4 st)

Rows 22–24: 4 sc, 1 ch, turn

Row 25: 2 sc, dec., 1 ch, turn (3 st)

Rows 26–27: 3 sc, 1 ch, turn

Row 28: SC in each stitch (3 st)

Cut the yarn and weave it in.

Insert the hook in row 8, in the stitch immediately next to the first tentacle, and repeat rows 9 to 28. Continue that way until you've worked all of row 8 and made eight tentacles.

Now that the bottom of the tentacles is done, you can start making the top part. Grab the blue yarn and start working directly after row 28. For a better understanding of how to connect your stitches to the bottom part of the tentacle, page 17.

Row 29: (blue) Inc., 1 sc, Inc., 1 sc in the edge stitch of row 26, turn (5 st)

Row 30: 5 sc, 1 sc in the edge stitch of row 25, turn

Row 31: 5 sc, 1 sc in the edge stitch of row 24, turn

Row 32: Inc., 4 sc, 1 sc in the edge stitch of row 23, turn (6 st)

Row 33: 6 sc, 1 sc in the edge stitch of row 22, turn

Row 34: 6 sc, 1 sc in the edge stitch of row 21, turn

Row 35: 6 sc, 1 sc in the edge stitch of row 20, turn

Row 36: 5 sc, Inc., 1 sc in the edge stitch of row 19, turn (7 st)

Side view

The body

Row 37: 7 sc, 1 sc in the edge stitch of row 18, turn

Row 38: 7 sc, 1 sc in the edge stitch of row 17, turn

Row 39: 7 sc, 1 sc in the edge stitch of row 16, turn

Row 40: Inc., 6 sc, 1 sc in the edge stitch of row 15, turn (8 st)

Row 41: 8 sc, 1 sc in the edge stitch of row 14, turn

Row 42: 8 sc, 1 sc in the edge stitch of row 13, turn

Row 43: 8 sc, 1 sc in the edge stitch of row 12, turn

Row 44: 7 sc, Inc., 1 sc in the edge stitch of row 11, turn (9 st)

Row 45: 9 sc, 1 sc in the edge stitch of row 10, turn

Row 46: 9 sc, 1 sc in the edge stitch of row 9, turn

Row 47: 9 sc, 1 sc in the edge stitch of row 8, turn

Row 48: 9 sc, 1 sc in the edge stitch of row 7

Cut the yarn and weave it in.

Repeat those steps seven more times to finish shaping the eight tentacles. Starting now, you'll resume working in the round to continue making the body.

Rnd 49: (blue) SC in each stitch around (72 st)

Stuff the tentacles.

Rnd 50: *7 sc, dec.* x 8 (64 st)

Rnd 51: *6 sc, dec.* x 8 (56 st)

Rnds 52–56: SC in each stitch around (56 st)

Rnd 57: *26 sc, dec.* x 2 (54 st)

Rnds 58–59: SC in each stitch around (54 st)

Rnd 60: *7 sc, dec.* x 6 (48 st)

Rnds 61–62: SC in each stitch around (48 st)

Rnd 63: 3 sc, dec., *6 sc, dec.* x 5, 3 sc (42 st)

Rnds 64–65: SC in each stitch around (42 st)

Rnd 66: *5 sc, dec.* x 6 (36 st)

Rnds 67–69: SC in each stitch around (36 st)

Rnd 70: 2 sc, dec., *4 sc, dec.* x 5, 2 sc (30 st)

Rnds 71–73: SC in each stitch around (30 st)

Attach the arms at round 71 (page 14) Stuff tightly. Finish with 1 sl st, then cut the yarn leaving enough length for sewing.

The back

The necktie

The cover

The pages

FINISHING

You should have enough yarn left after finishing the body to sew it to the head. Simply place the head on the opening of the body and finish stuffing tightly, then sew them together.

Sew the arms to the body around row 71 if you haven't already attached them.

THE NECKTIE

In gold

Row 1: 2 ch, turn
Row 2: Inc., 1 ch and turn (2 st)
Row 3: 2 Inc., 1 ch and turn (4 st)
Rows 4–9: 4 sc, 1 ch and turn (4 st)
Row 10: 1 sc, dec., 1 sc, 1 ch and turn (3 st)
Rows 11–13: 3 sc, 1 ch and turn (3 st)

Row 14: SC in each stitch (3 st)
Cut the yarn and weave it in. Make another piece the same way then attach them together, wrong sides facing each other, by crocheting one sc row all the way around (page 12). Make a chain long enough to wrap around the neck of the squid and sew the tie onto it.

BOOK

THE COVER

Worked flat in gold.

Row 1: 21 ch, turn
Rows 2–12: 20 sc, 1 ch, turn (20 st)
Row 13: SC in each stitch (20 st)
Crochet one sc row all around the rectangle for a pretty finish (page 12). Finish with a sl st, cut

the yarn and weave it in. You may embroider anything you'd like on the cover. I chose an N (a tip of the hat to H. P. Lovecraft's *Necronomicon*).

THE PAGES

In white

Row 1: 4 ch, turn
Rows 2–28: 3 sc, 1 ch, turn (3 st)
Row 29: SC in each stitch (3 st)
Keep a decent length of white yarn to sew your piece inside the cover. Stuff lightly, cut the yarn and weave it in.

Want even more creative content?

Visit us online at **ctpub.com**

Make it,
snap it,
share it

#ctpublishing